# ROCKY MOUNTAIN SPOTTED FEVER

DEADLY DISEASES AND EPIDEMICS

# ROCKY MOUNTAIN
# SPOTTED FEVER

## David H. Walker, M.D.

FOUNDING EDITOR
The Late I. Edward Alcamo
Distinguished Teaching Professor of Microbiology,
SUNY Farmingdale

FOREWORD BY
David Heymann
World Health Organization

CHELSEA HOUSE
PUBLISHERS
An imprint of Infobase Publishing

Chelsea House
An imprint of Infobase Publishing
132 West 31st Street
New York, NY 10001

**Library of Congress Cataloging-in-Publication Data**
Walker, David H., 1943–
    Rocky Mountain spotted fever / David H. Walker ; foreword by David Heymann.
       p. cm. — (Deadly diseases and epidemics)
    Includes bibliographical references and index.
    ISBN-13: 978-0-7910-8678-0 (acid-free paper)
    ISBN-10: 0-7910-8678-X (acid-free paper)   1. Rocky Mountain spotted fever—
Juvenile literature.   I. Heymann, David L. II. Title. III. Series.

    RC182.R6W35 2008
    616.9'223—dc22

                                                                        2007018549

Chelsea House books are available at special discounts when purchased in bulk quantities for businesses, associations, institutions, or sales promotions. Please call our Special Sales Department in New York at (212) 967-8800 or (800) 322-8755.

You can find Chelsea House on the World Wide Web at http://www.chelseahouse.com

Series design by Terry Mallon
Cover design by Keith Trego
Printed in the United States of America
Bang EJB 10 9 8 7 6 5 4 3 2 1
This book is printed on acid-free paper.

All links and Web addresses were checked and verified to be correct at the time of publication. Because of the dynamic nature of the Web, some addresses and links may have changed since publication and may no longer be valid.

# Table of Contents

# Foreword

In the 1960s, many of the infectious diseases that had terrorized generations were tamed. After a century of advances, the leading killers of Americans both young and old were being prevented with new vaccines or cured with new medicines. The risk of death from pneumonia, tuberculosis (TB), meningitis, influenza, whooping cough, and diphtheria declined dramatically. New vaccines lifted the fear that summer would bring polio, and a global campaign was on the verge of eradicating smallpox worldwide. New pesticides like DDT cleared mosquitoes from homes and fields, thus reducing the incidence of malaria, which was present in the southern United States and which remains a leading killer of children worldwide. New technologies produced safe drinking water and removed the risk of cholera and other water-borne diseases. Science seemed unstoppable. Disease seemed destined to all but disappear.

But the euphoria of the 1960s has evaporated.

The microbes fought back. Those causing diseases like TB and malaria evolved resistance to cheap and effective drugs. The mosquito developed the ability to defuse pesticides. New diseases emerged, including AIDS, Legionnaires', and Lyme disease. And diseases which had not been seen in decades reemerged, as the hantavirus did in the Navajo Nation in 1993. Technology itself actually created new health risks. The global transportation network, for example, meant that diseases like West Nile virus could spread beyond isolated regions and quickly become global threats. Even modern public health protections sometimes failed, as they did in 1993 in Milwaukee, Wisconsin, resulting in 400,000 cases of the digestive system illness cryptosporidiosis. And, more recently, the threat from smallpox, a disease believed to be completely eradicated, has returned along with other potential bioterrorism weapons such as anthrax.

The lesson is that the fight against infectious diseases will never end.

In our constant struggle against disease, we as individuals have a weapon that does not require vaccines or drugs, and that is the warehouse of knowledge. We learn from the history of science that

"modern" beliefs can be wrong. In this series of books, for example, you will learn that diseases like syphilis were once thought to be caused by eating potatoes. The invention of the microscope set science on the right path. There are more positive lessons from history. For example, smallpox was eliminated by vaccinating everyone who had come in contact with an infected person. This "ring" approach to smallpox control is still the preferred method for confronting an outbreak, should the disease be intentionally reintroduced.

At the same time, we are constantly adding new drugs, new vaccines, and new information to the warehouse. Recently, the entire human genome was decoded. So too was the genome of the parasite that causes malaria. Perhaps by looking at the microbe and the victim through the lens of genetics we will be able to discover new ways to fight malaria, which remains the leading killer of children in many countries.

Because of advances in our understanding of such diseases as AIDS, entire new classes of antiretroviral drugs have been developed. But resistance to all these drugs has already been detected, so we know that AIDS drug development must continue.

Education, experimentation, and the discoveries that grow out of them are the best tools to protect health. Opening this book may put you on the path of discovery. I hope so, because new vaccines, new antibiotics, new technologies, and, most importantly, new scientists are needed now more than ever if we are to remain on the winning side of this struggle against microbes.

David Heymann
Executive Director
Communicable Diseases Section
World Health Organization
Geneva, Switzerland

# 1

# What Is a Rickettsia?

The **causative** agent of Rocky Mountain spotted fever is a rickettsia, a bacterium known by the scientific name *Rickettsia rickettsii*. It is an unusual organism that has a very strange lifestyle. It survives by growing inside the cells of another living being, which is called its **host**. Some hosts of *Rickettsia rickettsii* are ticks and wild animals such as rodents. When humans or their dogs become infected, their cells are infected, leading to the life-threatening disease Rocky Mountain spotted fever.

Viewed at high magnification in an electron microscope, *Rickettsia rickettsii* are seen growing by one bacterium splitting into two bacteria. Scientists who study them can grow them in the laboratory, by breaking open infected cells, releasing the bacteria, and **inoculating** them into a flask containing healthy uninfected cells. *Rickettsia rickettsii* enters the uninfected cell and begins to multiply. If a scientist inoculates these rickettsiae onto a laboratory dish containing rich **agar** on which most ordinary bacteria grow, the rickettsiae do not grow. Indeed, outside of a host cell, they survive only a short while. For this reason, hospital laboratories cannot find *Rickettsia rickettsii* when they culture the blood of patients infected with Rocky Mountain spotted fever by inoculating agar culture plates. This obstacle to diagnosis also complicates research seeking to understand the bacteria themselves as well as how they make people sick.

As bacteria, rickettsiae contain both ribonucleic acid (RNA) and deoxyribonucleic acid (DNA), generate energy, secrete substances, and perform other living functions. Like nearly all bacteria they have a cell wall, and during growth they do not disassemble, but rather they double their genetic content and separate into two bacteria with the same amount of DNA encoding all the genes in both progeny cells. They have 800-1,400

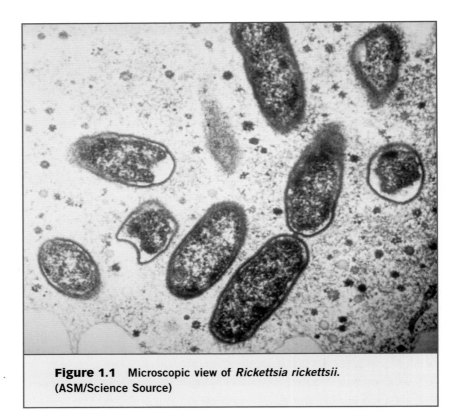

**Figure 1.1**  Microscopic view of *Rickettsia rickettsii*.
(ASM/Science Source)

genes that encode many life functions. Bacteria life functions can generally be inhibited by antibiotics, and rickettsiae are vulnerable to some antibiotics. They have a common type of cell wall known as **Gram negative**.

## ORIGIN OF THE NAME *RICKETTSIA*

The most important scientist in the early studies of Rocky Mountain spotted fever was Dr. Howard Ricketts, a young medical doctor who devoted his life to the investigation of infectious diseases. In 1906, he traveled from his home in Chicago to the frontier of western Montana to search for the cause of a disease that broke out there every spring and killed most of those who became ill with it. Working in a tent set up on the

grounds of a hospital in Bitterroot Valley, he showed that infection could be transferred from the blood of infected patients to guinea pigs that he had brought with him on the train. The infection could also be passed from ticks to guinea pigs. Once they recovered from the infection, guinea pigs were **immune** to the **agent**. Suspecting that ticks transmitted the infection, Dr. Ricketts examined them in his microscope and saw unusually small rod-shaped bacteria within their body fluid cells. Over the next three years, he worked for long hours and designed many creative studies. The Rocky Mountain spotted fever organisms were named *Rickettsia rickettsii* in his honor years after his premature death in 1910 in Mexico City, where he was on the verge of finding the causative agent of typhus fever. The typhus agent was named *Rickettsia prowazekii* in honor of him and Stanislaus von Prowazek, who also died of a typhus fever infection acquired during his laboratory research.

## THE LANGUAGE OF BACTERIOLOGY

Many scientific names are in classical Latin or Greek. For persons who are not scholars of these ancient languages, the various forms of the scientific terms can be confusing because their endings change in ways that differ from English. Scientists are scholars too, and take pride in using the correct form of the words. For example, *bacterium* (based on a Greek word) is singular. The plural form is *bacteria*. Thus, a precise scientist would say, "The bacteria are growing," not "the bacteria is growing."

Rickettsia (based on a feminine Latin word) is singular, and the plural form is rickettsiae. Thus, one might observe that a cell contains many rickettsiae. The second word in the species name *Rickettsia rickettsii* is the possessive form of the Latin word meaning *of* Ricketts or Ricketts'; that is, the "rickettsia of Ricketts," the first one discovered by him in his tent in Montana.

**Figure 1.2**   Howard Ricketts. (U.S. National Library of Medicine)

## A METHOD TO GROW RICKETTSIAE IS DISCOVERED

By 1938, the United States Public Health Service had established a laboratory in the Bitterroot Valley and was producing a vaccine against Rocky Mountain spotted fever. Because a technique for growing rickettsiae in the laboratory had not been

found, the vaccine was produced from infected ticks. Batches of ticks served as culture vessels of *Rickettsia rickettsii*. The ticks infected themselves by feeding on rickettsia-containing blood sucked from the skin of experimentally infected guinea pigs. The infected ticks were ground up, and the rickettsiae in this product were inactivated chemically so that they could not grow in the vaccinated person. This manufacturing process was difficult and dangerous. Some brave workers died of the infection that they caught in the laboratory while preparing a vaccine to protect others. The crude vaccine was not entirely effective. Vaccinated persons sometimes became ill, but a much higher proportion survived than patients who had not received the vaccine.

A young scientist in the Rocky Mountain Laboratory in Hamilton, Montana, Dr. Herald Cox, was attempting to develop a better method for growing rickettsiae. Tissue culture or cell culture is the growth of cells outside of the body in a flask or tube. The cells must be maintained in a fluid that contains all the necessary nutrients at an appropriate level of acid-base balance, temperature, and other factors. Even under ideal conditions, scientists in that era did not have effective methods to prevent contamination by everyday environmental bacteria and fungi. Dr. Cox was working to prepare cell cultures from the embryos in chicken eggs, but his efforts were plagued by unwanted growth of contaminants. Ultimately he devised a method to inoculate rickettsiae through the shell of the egg directly into the sterile yolk sac. It worked! At the optimal temperature for the rickettsiae (34°C), the bacteria grew in the cells of the yolk sac. After several days, the embryo died and the yolk sac containing millions of rickettsiae could be harvested. A better source of these organisms became available for vaccines and for research.

## EVOLUTION OF RICKETTSIAE

The ancient ancestors of rickettsiae were free-living bacteria. Rickettsiae and **mitochondria**, a cellular **organelle** that

**Figure 1.3**  Dr. Herald Cox inoculating eggs with rickettsiae. (U.S. National Library of Medicine)

produces energy, share a common bacterial ancestor from which they evolved over tens of millions of years. Mitochondria became entirely adapted to the cells in which they live; they cannot survive without the cell, and the cell cannot survive without them.

In a similar way, rickettsiae have adapted to life inside the cell. They cannot survive outside host cells where they can grow. The **cytosol**, or fluid interior, of the host cell is rich in nutrients, building blocks for growth, and energy-containing chemicals. Rickettsiae evolved transport mechanisms to acquire these substances from the host cell and thus no longer needed their own machinery to manufacture them. The genes that coded for this machinery in rickettsiae degraded. The

rickettsial complete set of genes diminished until it became only one-fourth that of ordinary bacteria. Rickettsiae lost the ability to live outside of the cell, but they had gained the ability to use the environment inside the cell much more effectively than ordinary bacteria.

Rickettsiae are smaller than most other bacteria, 0.3 micron by 1 micron (compared with 1 by 3 microns for ordinary bacteria). A micron equals one-millionth of a meter. For the purpose of comparison, a human hair is 100 microns in diameter, while the diameter of a human cell is normally several microns. The cell wall composition of rickettsiae resembles that of ordinary Gram-negative bacteria.

## THE FAMILY TREE OF RICKETTSIAE

*Rickettsia rickettsii* has a number of relatives. Many cause diseases throughout the world, such as *Rickettsia conorii* (Mediterranean spotted fever), *Rickettsia africae* (African tick bite fever), *Rickettsia sibirica* (north Asian tick typhus), *Rickettsia akari* (rickettsialpox), *Rickettsia japonica* (Japanese spotted fever), *Rickettsia australis* (Queensland tick typhus), *Rickettsia honei* (Flinders Island spotted fever), *Rickettsia prowazekii* (epidemic louse-borne typhus), and *Rickettsia typhi* (murine typhus). Others live in ticks or insects and appear not to cause any illness in humans, such as *Rickettsia bellii*, *Rickettsia peacockii*, and *Rickettsia montanensis*.

In summary, a rickettsiologist (the type of microbiologist who studies rickettsiae) would define these microorganisms as a group of genetically related, **obligately** intracellular bacteria that have evolved in association with an **arthropod vector**. The translation of this definition is that rickettsiae are closely related bacteria that must live inside a host cell and have a life cycle that involves, at some period of time, residing in a tick, louse, flea, or mite.

# 2

# The Amazing Life of a Tick

Most people find ticks disgusting. Even some medical students, who are more accustomed than the general public to seeing gory sights, really squirm when they see a close-up photograph of a tick crawling on someone's skin. Yet study of ticks reveals how interesting they actually are. To understand the bacteria that cause Rocky Mountain spotted fever, it's important to understand ticks, because that is where the bacteria have adapted to live.

## ARTHROPODS: HARD TICKS, SOFT TICKS, MITES, SPIDERS, AND INSECTS

Ticks come in two main types, hard ticks and soft ticks. Hard ticks spread the germs that cause Rocky Mountain spotted fever. Their body is covered by a hard outer structure that protects the soft inner organs. As with other arthropods, this outer surface contains a substance called chitin, which gives the tick its shape. The shape, color, and patterns on the shell enable specialists to identify the species of the tick. Scientists who are experts on arthropods are called entomologists, and those who specialize in ticks are acarologists.

Ticks differ from insects. Adult ticks have eight legs; adult insects have only six legs. Ticks are not the only eight-legged arthropods. Spiders and adult mites also have four pairs of legs and are closer relatives to ticks than to insects.

Five species of ticks transmit *Rickettsia rickettsii*: *Dermacentor variabilis* (the American dog tick), *Dermacentor andersoni* (the Rocky Mountain wood tick), *Rhipicephalus sanguineus* (the brown dog tick), *Amblyomma*

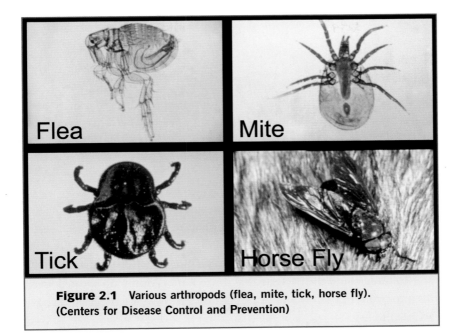

**Figure 2.1**   Various arthropods (flea, mite, tick, horse fly). (Centers for Disease Control and Prevention)

*cajennense* (the cayenne tick), and *Amblyomma aureolatum* (the yellow dog tick). The two *Dermacentor* ticks appear very similar to the naked eye, as do the two *Amblyomma* ticks. Special sets of specific features, called keys, are observed under a microscope to identify each species.

The key that determines the identity of *Dermacentor variabilis* includes several technical characteristics of the length and shape of particular microscopic tick body parts, such as the coxal spurs, the spiracular plate, and the cornua length. These features differentiate it from the remaining eight species that are present in the United States. Thus, the specific identification of the species should be performed by tick taxonomists, who are experts in identifying ticks. It is important to realize that there are many species of tick. Some carry other diseases such as *Ixodes scapularis*, which transmits Lyme disease, and many other tick species that do not carry germs that infect humans.

## TICK FEEDING

Ticks are stealthy creatures. People generally find a tick on their body by seeing it, feeling it walk over their skin, or touching an attached tick with their fingers and investigating it. Tick bites do not hurt because ticks inject a chemical that destroys an important substance the human body uses to register pain. An adult tick feeds for more than a week before becoming **satiated**, detaching, and falling to the ground, where it finds refuge. The person or animal may never know that a tick was attached to its skin. This is very different from the blood meal taken in seconds by a mosquito that is painful and leaves an irritating itch.

Other aspects of tick feeding differ from suck-and-fly insects. At the beginning of the meal, the tick inserts

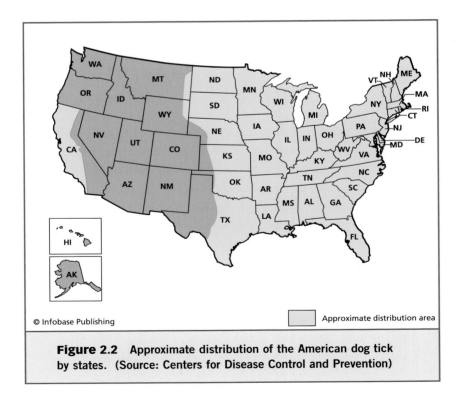

© Infobase Publishing

Approximate distribution area

**Figure 2.2** Approximate distribution of the American dog tick by states. (Source: Centers for Disease Control and Prevention)

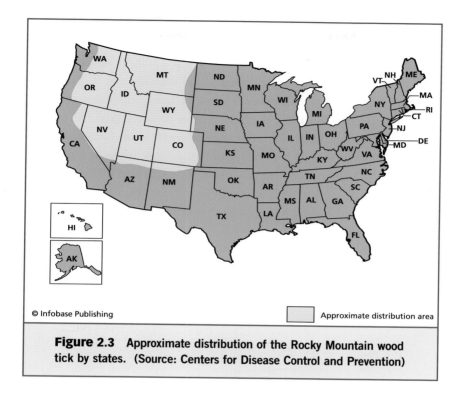

**Figure 2.3** Approximate distribution of the Rocky Mountain wood tick by states. (Source: Centers for Disease Control and Prevention)

sharp mouthparts into the skin and uses them to cut blood vessels, creating a small blood-filled space under the surface. Normally the human body would respond by stopping the blood flow into the wound by clotting the blood in the damaged blood vessel. Tick saliva injected into the skin contains substances that stop blood coagulation, allowing a tick to keep the blood flowing for more than a week while it feeds. Platelets fail to form a clot and the blood continues to flow.

Unlike a mosquito bite, a tick bite typically shows no signs of inflammation; it does not become red, swollen, painful, or itchy. At the site of tick feeding, a hidden battle takes place. The host's immune and inflammatory defenses fight the chemicals in the tick's saliva that have been injected into the skin to inhibit these very defenses. Ticks have evolved these evasive abilities over eons. Their life depends on the

## THE LIFE CYCLE OF A HARD TICK

The life cycle of hard ticks has three stages, not counting the egg: larva, nymph, and adult. The tick egg hatches, and the smallest form, called a larva, emerges. It has only six legs and is the size of a pinhead. Most people would not recognize it as a tick. The larva may not get an opportunity to feed for weeks, months, or longer. Eventually, it must feed on blood from a small animal or die. After engorging on blood, it drops off the animal and molts. It sheds its hard exoskeleton and grows a different, larger outer covering and eight legs. The tick is now in the second, or nymphal, stage. A nymph also waits for the chance to feed. When it too has fed to repletion and dropped off its host animal, it molts to become the large adult form that nearly everyone recognizes as a tick. Each stage is capable of surviving a long time without a meal, even up to a few years for adults. Adult ticks are differentiated sexually into males and females, which mate during the third and last blood meal of the tick's lifetime. After the blood-filled female with fertilized eggs detaches from the large or medium-sized animal and drops to the ground, she will lay thousands of eggs, and the life cycle that might have taken one to five years to complete begins again.

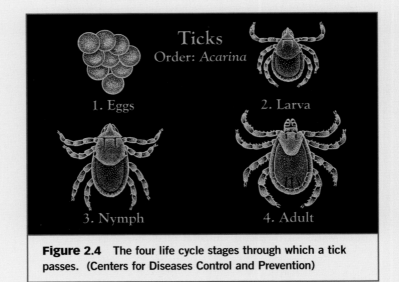

**Figure 2.4** The four life cycle stages through which a tick passes. (Centers for Diseases Control and Prevention)

## A BIRDSEYE VIEW OF TICKS

Clarence Birdseye was born in Brooklyn, New York, and lacked the money to complete his education at Amherst College. He left and headed west to seek his fortune. In 1910, he noted an abundance of ticks on the hides of a bear and three mountain goats, important hosts of the tick *Dermacentor andersoni*, the vector of *Rickettsia rickettsii* in the Rocky Mountains. Birdseye participated in the collection of more than 700 animals in western Montana, which showed that 18 species were infested with these ticks. These animals play a role in the life cycle of ticks. Understanding the ticks is knowledge that could potentially allow their control and thus, indirectly the control of the rickettsiae living within them. One approach was dipping tick-infested cattle into solutions that contained substances that poisoned the ticks.

Later, while in the fur-trading business in Labrador in Canada, Birdseye noticed the Inuit's method of preserving food by quickly freezing it and once again put his perception to good use. The Inuit technique maintained the best flavor, texture, and color of the food. Birdseye adapted it to start a business, and today the Birdseye name is found in frozen food departments of grocery stores everywhere. Observation and creativity are useful in both science and business.

three blood feasts of their lifetime and they have adapted well to this lifestyle.

### THIRSTY TICKS

Imagine living for a couple of years and only imbibing a liquid three times. Severe dehydration would be inevitable for most organisms, but not for ticks. Their hard covering protects them from surface loss of water by evaporation. Furthermore, they obtain water through an unusual strategy. They secrete salt

onto their mouthparts. The salt attracts water from humid air, and droplets form on the mouthparts by a process known as deliquescence. The tick then swallows these droplets, replenishing its water stores.

Ticks face the opposite challenge when feeding on blood. There is more water in blood than a tick can use. In fact, a tick must concentrate the nutrients by getting rid of the excess water. It accomplishes this feat using another special function of its salivary glands, the ability to pump water back into the animal's skin. The tick keeps the nutrients and blood needed to feed. The **engorged** tick has actually taken even more blood than its impressive size would suggest because the blood is in a very concentrated form. An adult hard tick may grown 200 to 600 times its normal size after feeding. Once detached from

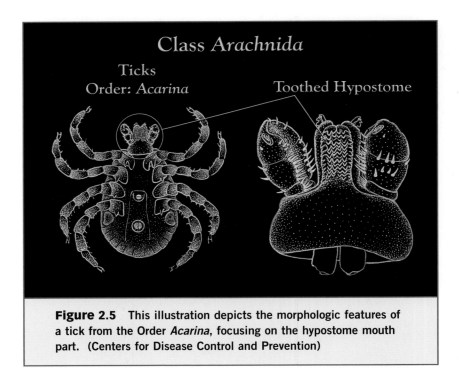

**Figure 2.5** This illustration depicts the morphologic features of a tick from the Order *Acarina*, focusing on the hypostome mouth part. (Centers for Disease Control and Prevention)

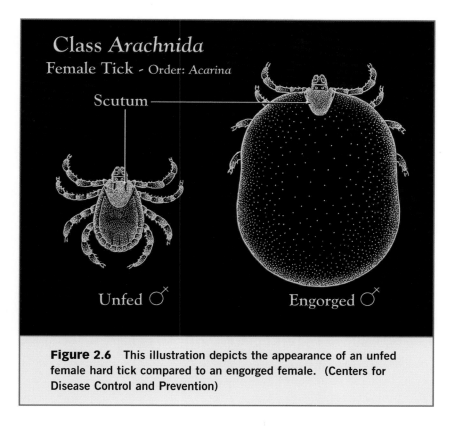

**Figure 2.6**  This illustration depicts the appearance of an unfed female hard tick compared to an engorged female.  (Centers for Disease Control and Prevention)

the animal host, a tick must shift gears from water diversion to water conservation since it may not feed again for a very long time. Ticks feed very few times over the course of their relatively short life span.

The next chapter will explain the role that the tick and its lifestyle play in the survival of *Rickettsia rickettsii* in nature.

# 3

# The Natural Ecology of
# *Rickettsia rickettsii*

Rocky Mountain spotted fever occurs when a tick injects *R. rickettsii* into a person's skin during its blood meal. Epidemiology is the specific study of the who (e.g., age, gender), when, and where a particular disease occurs. The **epidemiology** of this disease is determined by the factors that lead to the encounter between infected ticks and humans.

For a tick to transmit the infection, it must carry the germs. In nature, fewer than 1 in 1,000 ticks belonging to the tick species that can transmit *R. rickettsii* actually have these bacteria in them. This fact explains why few tick bites result in Rocky Mountain spotted fever.

The main means by which these rickettsiae are maintained in nature is their passage from one generation to the next via infected tick eggs. The ovaries of the female tick become infected and pass on the bacteria. This mechanism is called **transovarian transmission**, and it can carry *R. rickettsii* through several generations of ticks. The larval tick that hatches from the infected egg also carries the rickettsiae. When larvae molt to nymphs, and nymphs molt to adult ticks, the rickettsiae are passed onward to the next stage, leading to another batch of infected eggs.

## HOW *RICKETTSIA RICKETTSII*
## ENTER UNINFECTED TICKS

It is not surprising that bacteria that cause a severe human disease would also injure their other hosts, including ticks. After several generations, rickettsial growth to high concentrations in ticks causes

**Figure 3.1**  American Dog Tick engorged and feeding on dog's ear. (Noah Poritz/Photo Researchers, Inc.)

fewer eggs to be produced and causes reduced survival of larvae and subsequent tick stages. If this process were not balanced by another factor, the rickettsiae would destroy the host in which they must live, and they would disappear from the Earth.

This other factor is the establishment of new lines of infected ticks. When infected ticks feed on an animal, *R. rickettsii* are injected into the skin, and invade the animal's blood. Later, uninfected ticks suck infected blood into their gut. The rickettsiae in the infected animal's blood invade the cells of the wall of the tick's intestine, where they establish the infection.

Not all infectious agents that enter the intestine of a tick during its feeding on infected blood can pass through the wall of the gut. This gut barrier cannot stop *R. rickettsii*. The germs spread into the tick's body cavity, salivary glands, and ovaries.

Then this tick lays infected eggs and injects rickettsiae into other animal in its saliva during the next blood meal.

## EPIDEMIOLOGY OF ROCKY MOUNTAIN SPOTTED FEVER

Rocky Mountain spotted fever is a seasonal disease. This infection occurs only rarely during the cold winter months. In the southeastern and south-central United States, cases begin to occur in May and continue until September. This is the time when ticks emerge from their cold weather hiding places and begin looking for an animal to provide them a blood meal. People love to go outdoors in spring and summer, and it is inevitable that they encounter ticks, and rickettsiae are transmitted.

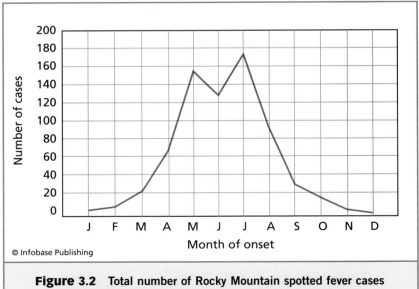

© Infobase Publishing

**Figure 3.2**  Total number of Rocky Mountain spotted fever cases by month of onset during 2002, as determined on the basis of case report forms submitted by the states to the Centers for Disease Control and Prevention. (Source: Centers for Disease Control and Prevention)

Historically, Rocky Mountain spotted fever has always had a high **incidence** in children. Kids enjoy playing outside the house and have more free time after school and during summer vacation than adults do. Many of them spend time with dogs or other pets. Dogs are a favored host of the American dog tick, *Dermacentor variabilis*, the most important vector of Rocky Mountain spotted fever in the United States. Presumably, these factors explain why children are at greater risk of getting the disease.

In recent years, the incidence of Rocky Mountain spotted fever has increased to high levels in adults of retirement age. This segment of the population has increased, and older adults spend greater amounts of leisure time fishing, hunting, gardening, and in other outdoor activities where encounters with ticks occur. Perhaps this situation may explain their increased risk of Rocky Mountain spotted fever.

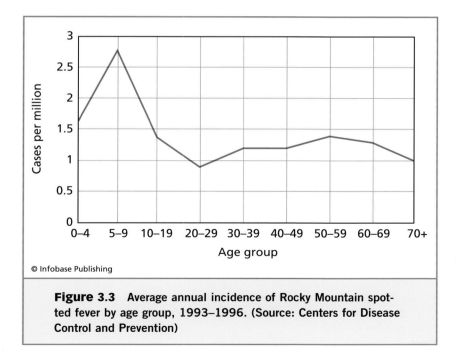

© Infobase Publishing

**Figure 3.3** Average annual incidence of Rocky Mountain spotted fever by age group, 1993–1996. (Source: Centers for Disease Control and Prevention)

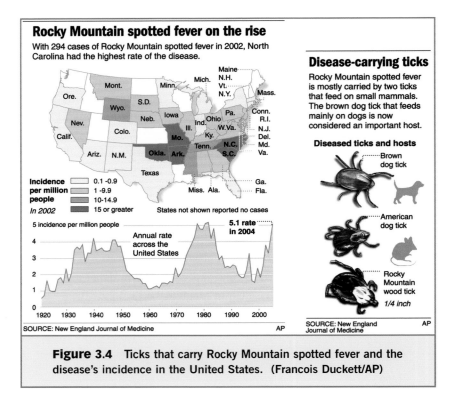

**Figure 3.4** Ticks that carry Rocky Mountain spotted fever and the disease's incidence in the United States. (Francois Duckett/AP)

Although Rocky Mountain spotted fever occurs throughout the United States, with the exception of Vermont and Hawaii, it has its highest incidence in the warm, humid Southern states. Most of the tick vectors do not thrive in the dry climate of the desert Southwestern states, and the distribution of the American dog tick stops at a northern limit that is most likely determined by a combination of cold and dryness. Some areas of Vermont, the inland portion of Maine, and the southern inland area of Canada are considered to be the "northern limit" for the American dog tick. The longer Southern warm season correlates with a longer season of transmission. In the area of high incidence in western Montana, the season of the Rocky Mountain wood tick is short and it is fierce in its search for a blood meal.

## CYCLES OF EMERGENCE AND RE-EMERGENCE

From time to time, physicians and public health doctors note the presence of a disease that they do not recognize. Usually, it has been there all along but was unrecognized. When epidemiologic factors lead to increased numbers of infections or science develops methods to identify the agent, a new infectious disease is discovered. In reality, during the past 40 years, on average, more than one new infectious agent has been identified per year. Such a new disease is referred to as an emerging infectious disease. This is a phenomenon that was defined only recently, but has been occurring for much longer.

Rocky Mountain spotted fever was first reported by a frontier Army doctor in the 1870s and was described in detail in an article written by a physician in Idaho in 1899. Since then, there have been two long cycles of increased numbers of cases

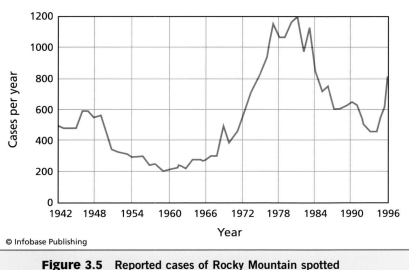

© Infobase Publishing

**Figure 3.5** Reported cases of Rocky Mountain spotted fever in the United States, 1942–1996. (Source: Centers for Disease Control and Prevention)

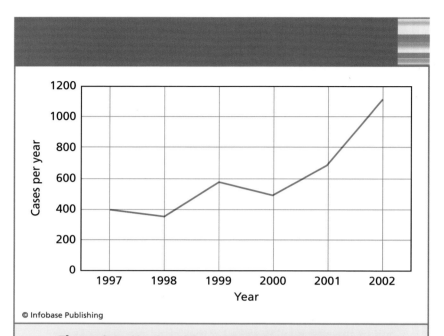

© Infobase Publishing

**Figure 3.6**   Number of Rocky Mountain spotted fever cases in the United States, 1997–2002, as determined by the number of cases reported to the Centers for Disease Control and Prevention by the states via the National Electronic Tele-communications System for Surveillance (NETSS). (Source: Centers for Disease Control and Prevention)

followed by decreased incidence. There was a period of high incidence in the Western United States during the first half of the twentieth century, followed by a dramatic decrease in mid-century. After reaching a low point around 1960, the incidence began to rise again, particularly in the southeastern and south-central states. By the early 1970s, public health attention was called to the alarming increase in number of cases, which reached a peak incidence in the early 1980s and then began to decline again. Clues suggestive of another re-emergence are occurring again at the time of the publication of this book.

*(continues)*

*(continued)*

What determines these seemingly unstoppable waves of Rocky Mountain spotted fever? Speculation during the previous crest included people building new houses and moving into places that ticks live, increases in outdoor recreational activities, and other phenomena that continued as the incidence subsequently fell. They were not the explanation for the changing incidence. Other rickettsial diseases in different parts of the world have similar waves of increased incidence, sometimes occurring simultaneously with that of Rocky Mountain spotted fever. Science awaits studies of nature and of laboratory experiments that will determine the underlying cause of this re-emergence and perhaps even propose a method for its control. Interference by nondisease-causing rickettsiae and by the effects of *R. rickettsii* that harm infected ticks are likely contributors to the rise and fall, but no mathematical model yet exists to explain the epidemiology of Rocky Mountain spotted fever.

The most critical factor in the equation defining the risk of human infection is the number of active ticks carrying *R. rickettsii*. In part, this number depends on the total population of vector ticks, which seems to vary throughout each warm season and annually. Likely determinants of the tick population (which of course never undergoes a real census) are levels of humidity and availability of animal hosts suitable for providing blood meals at the different tick stages. The animal populations may also depend upon rainfall and its effects on their food supplies. Not all of the critical animal hosts of the ticks are known, but small rodents and deer are important. Larger populations of particular animals may support the survival of larger populations of ticks.

Another factor is the proportion of ticks that are infected with *R. rickettsii*. It has been shown experimentally that cotton rats (*Sigmodon hispidus*) can be infected with *R. rickettsii* by tick bite and can serve as a source of *R. rickettsii* for uninfected ticks that feed on these animals while rickettsiae are in their blood.

# 4

# Rocky Mountain Spotted Fever: Course and Clinical Features

Nearly half of the people who develop Rocky Mountain spotted fever are unaware of having a tick bite or do not recall it. In some rural and suburban locations, finding ticks crawling on or attached to one's skin is a common event, frequently taken for granted. Because so few ticks carry *Rickettsia rickettsii*, there is seldom a bad consequence of any particular tick bite.

When a tick inoculates disease-causing rickettsiae into the skin during feeding, the person continues to feel healthy for about a week. Then the illness begins, often abruptly. The time interval between the tick's injection of bacteria into the skin and the patient's first symptom is called the incubation period of the disease and is discussed in more detail in the next chapter.

## EARLY COURSE OF ILLNESS

At the onset of illness, the patient feels unwell and often has shaking chills, after which there is a feverish sensation. Over the next day or two, the fever rises to a higher level, and the person experiences what is often described as the worst headache ever. Other symptoms that occur frequently are muscle aches, loss of appetite, nausea, vomiting, and pain in the abdomen.

These clinical manifestations occur with many diseases, including some common viral infections. Unlike many of those infections, however,

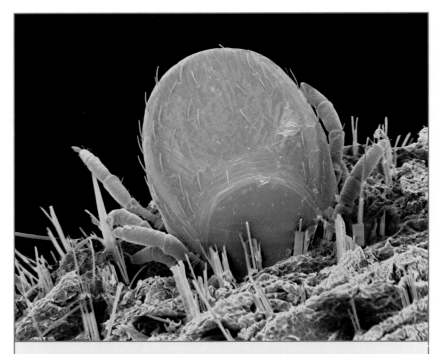

**Figure 4.1**  Colored scanning electron micrograph of a tick feeding head-down in human skin.  (Volker Steger/Photo Researchers, Inc.)

Rocky Mountain spotted fever does not resolve with only a few days of bed rest. In fact, the clinical signs and symptoms worsen progressively day after day. By the second or third day of illness, most patients decide that they need to be examined by a medical doctor. Often the patient will have to return to the doctor's office or visit an emergency room one or more times if the correct diagnosis is not suspected. Patients are often treated initially with antibiotics that would kill other common disease-causing bacteria but have no effect on *Rickettsia rickettsii*. Most people with Rocky Mountain spotted fever become so ill that they must be admitted to a hospital for medical treatment and nursing care.

## THE DEVELOPMENT OF A RASH AND
## ITS PROGRESSIVE CHANGES

Ninety percent of people with Rocky Mountain spotted fever will develop a rash. The rash is not present at the beginning of the illness. In half of patients with Rocky Mountain spotted fever, the rash does not appear until after the third day of illness; though in some cases it has appeared on the first or second day of illness. Typically, the first evidence of the rash is faint pink spots that are one to three millimeters in diameter and are located on the wrists or ankles. Over the next day or

## OTHER SOURCES OF
## *RICKETTSIA RICKETTSII* INFECTIONS

The vast majority of patients with Rocky Mountain spotted fever are infected when ticks inject *Rickettsia rickettsii* into their skin along with secretions of their salivary glands during feeding. Rickettsiae, however, can enter the body by other routes.

Removing ticks from a person or dog can be done safely, but crushing the tick can release rickettsiae from its body. If the person handling the tick contaminates a cut in the skin with tick juices, the rickettsiae can enter the patient via the skin wound and initiate an infection. If the infected tick fluids are present on one's fingers when the eye is rubbed, rickettsial infection can be introduced. People have even been infected while squeezing a tick when the tick's fluid squirted into their eye.

From late in the incubation period until near recovery, *Rickettsia rickettsii* are in the blood of the person. On at least one occasion, a person who felt well donated blood to a blood bank and soon thereafter developed Rocky Mountain spotted fever. Unfortunately, the blood already contained the bacteria at the time of the donation. The hospitalized patient who received the transfusion developed an unexplained febrile

so, more of these flat spots, called **macules**, appear on the arms and legs, and later on the chest, abdomen, and back. The spots progressively darken in color and become slightly raised above the level of the surrounding skin. The pink-to-red color of these spots is caused by localized areas of dilation of small blood vessels filled with red blood cells, like many tiny blushes. The slight elevation of the red spot is caused by leakage of fluid from the blood vessels into the skin. The raised spot is called a maculopapule. If the doctor presses on the macule or maculopapule at this stage of illness, the blood is squeezed out

illness that, despite no exposure to ticks, was Rocky Mountain spotted fever.

On another occasion, a medical doctor caring for a patient with Rocky Mountain spotted fever accidentally stuck himself with a needle that had been used to collect a blood sample from the patient. After an incubation period, the young doctor developed Rocky Mountain spotted fever, apparently from contamination of the needlestick with the patient's rickettsiae-laden blood.

People who do research with *Rickettsia rickettsii* must work in laboratories with special facilities and work procedures to prevent and contain aerosols of rickettsiae that are generated by routine laboratory procedures. These labs are labeled biosafety level 3 labs. Before these facilities and procedures were developed, many rickettsiologists were infected by breathing tiny aerosol particles into their lungs. Currently, any scientist who is not properly careful with samples containing *Rickettsia rickettsii* is also at risk of infection by inhaling unseen rickettsiae from the air. This danger is the basis for the potential misuse of these bacteria by terrorists as an aerosol bioweapon.

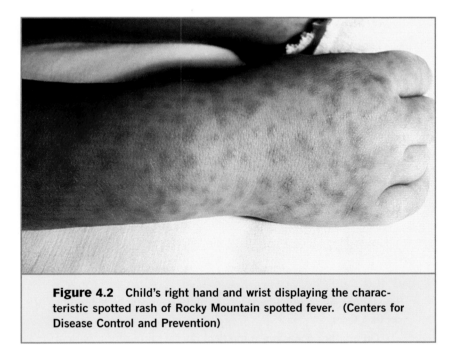

**Figure 4.2**   Child's right hand and wrist displaying the characteristic spotted rash of Rocky Mountain spotted fever. (Centers for Disease Control and Prevention)

of the network of blood vessels, and the spot blanches to the normal skin color.

In the half of patients whose disease progresses to an even more serious condition, a tiny hemorrhage appears in the center of the maculopapules. This darker spotted appearance of the skin is what gives Rocky Mountain spotted fever its name. If the rash is compressed by a finger's pressure at this point, the spot will not blanch because blood has escaped from the blood vessels into the skin tissue and cannot flow away. Whether or not a rash is present and how it looks depends on how far along the course of the illness has progressed.

## SIMILAR EVENTS OCCUR THROUGHOUT THE BODY

Damage similar to that seen on the skin is developing unseen inside the body. Two vital organs are particularly prone to life-threatening harm in Rocky Mountain spotted fever: the

lungs and brain. In severe cases, just as fluid leaks into the skin spots, small blood vessels leak water into the spaces in the lungs that should be filled with air. The abnormal accumulation of water outside of the blood vessels is known in medical terminology as **edema**. In the skin, edema is of little consequence. In the air spaces of the lungs, however, edema prevents the exchange of oxygen and carbon dioxide between the blood and the inhaled air. The oxygen concentration in the blood can fall to low levels, and organs, such as the brain, are deprived of this essential substance.

The chest radiograph of such a patient shows a whiter color in involved areas due to the greater density of water than the usual air-filled lungs. Listening to the infected patient's chest with a stethoscope, the medical doctor hears a sound similar to crumpling cellophane paper, the result of some of the fluid-filled airspaces overcoming the surface tension and popping open. It is a bad sign. If this process is not stopped by the immune system and antibiotics, this fluid in the lungs will drown the patient.

The damage in the brain, like that in the rash and the lungs, involves the small-sized blood vessels (capillaries, venules, and arterioles). The characteristic clinical result is confusion of the mind that can lead to a state of stupor. In the 10 percent of patients who are the most gravely ill and at the greatest risk of dying, the brain involvement advances to a coma. Many of these patients also suffer seizures with involuntary muscle contractions shaking their entire body.

Because so much fluid is lost from the inside of the blood vessels into the tissues as edema, the actual volume of the blood is reduced. Lacking sufficient blood volume for the heart to pump, the patient's blood pressure decreases, and the organs do not receive enough blood flow to supply their needs.

## OUTCOME OF THE ILLNESS

If not treated with an effective antibiotic, 20 percent to 25 percent of patients with Rocky Mountain spotted fever will

## THE CONTINUING DISCOVERY OF RICKETTSIAL DISEASES

More than 60 years ago, R.R. Parker reported the discovery of a new spotted fever rickettsia in the Gulf Coast tick (*Amblyomma maculatum*). Eventually the organism was named *Rickettsia parkeri* in honor of Dr. Parker, who had been the driving force and director of the Rocky Mountain Laboratory in Montana for many years before his death.

When I moved to the Gulf Coast of Texas in 1987, I began thinking about whether there were any undiscovered rickettsial diseases in the area. I knew that *Rickettsii parkeri* caused a febrile illness in experimentally infected guinea pigs and wondered if it also caused illness in humans. I prepared a grant application to investigate this hypothesis, but at the time it was rejected as uninteresting and unimportant by the review panel. During the past few years, however, scientists at the Centers for Disease Control and Prevention demonstrated that *Rickettsia parkeri* causes human infection with an eschar (a scar or scab) at the site of the tick bite, fever, rash, and swollen lymph nodes. A similar disease has been associated with *Rickettsia parkeri* transmitted by *Amblyomma triste* ticks in Uruguay, and *Rickettsia parkeri* has been identified in ticks in Brazil. It is conceivable that this rickettsial illness has existed undiscovered throughout the Americas for millennia.

What other diseases that can be treated effectively with antibiotics await identification? We have found that many patients in Mexico suspected clinically to have dengue fever, which is caused by a mosquito-transmitted virus, actually have rickettsial infections. Similarly, many patients in Cameroon initially thought to have malaria or typhoid fever were shown on careful investigation to have African tick bite fever caused by *Rickettsiae africae*. There are probably many more ill, infected persons in parts of the world where there are no rickettsiologists investigating the causes of acute fevers.

die. Untreated, Rocky Mountain spotted fever varies from moderately severe to fatal. In the average fatal case, death occurs on the 11th day of illness. There is an uncommon form of the disease, however, known as fulminant Rocky Mountain spotted fever, in which death occurs within the first five days of illness.

On the other hand, even without treatment with an appropriate antibiotic, at least 75 percent of patients recover. Recovery is usually complete, although weakness may persist for a month. A small proportion of patients develop gangrene of the fingers, hands, toes, feet, or legs, which may have to be amputated. In others, damage to the brain is permanent, leaving residual neurologic deficits such as paralysis, deafness or blindness.

# 5

# How Does Rickettsia Cause the Disease?

Many steps take place between the time that a tick injects *Rickettsia rickettsii* into a person's skin and when the individual first becomes ill. This interval during which the disease develops is known as the incubation period, such as the time between when an egg is laid and it hatches. By the time the patient begins to feel feverish and suffers headache and muscle aches, usually a week after the tick bite, the rickettsiae have spread throughout the body via the bloodstream and entered the **endothelial cells** that line the blood vessels in every organ.

The earliest events in the patient's skin where the rickettsiae enter the body have not been determined. For example, what type of cells the rickettsiae infect first is not known. There are numerous types of cells in the skin, including endothelial cells lining small blood vessels, **macrophages**, and **dendritic cells**. The latter two types of cells are **phagocytes** that can engulf the rickettsiae. Ironically, this ordinarily effective defense mechanism could benefit the rickettsiae, which are able to grow only inside the host's cells.

It is not known how the rickettsiae spread from the skin to the bloodstream. Although it is conceivable that they enter the blood vessels in the skin directly, it would seem more likely that they are carried by dendritic cells or macrophages into lymphatic vessels that lead from the skin to lymph nodes in the region of the tick bite. Lymph is a fluid that carries white blood cells throughout the body and it passes through lymph nodes. Lymph from the arm and hand, for example, drains into lymph nodes in the armpit on the same side of the body. The lymph nodes are part of the immune system and may be where

the development of protective immunity is initiated. Lymph from the area of the bite would contain some of the rickettsiae and would pass through the lymph node. Eventually it would enter a large vein. Thereafter, the rickettsiae would be pumped along with the blood to the lungs, brain, liver, spleen, kidneys, heart, and other organs.

## THE TARGET CELL OF RICKETTSIAL INFECTION

The key to understanding how *Rickettsia rickettsii* causes its deadly disease is the knowledge that it grows mainly in the **endothelium**. The endothelial cells that line all blood vessels are located at the interface between the blood and the surrounding tissues. They stand guard so that blood does not escape or hemorrhage. They mediate the transfer of nutrients and oxygen from the blood to the organs and the transfer of metabolic waste products from the organs to the blood. They must maintain unimpeded flow, deliver hormones, and assure a fluid balance. If they are extensively damaged and do not function properly, the consequences can be catastrophic.

## RICKETTSIAE INVADE THE TARGET CELL
## AND USE ITS MACHINERY

Rickettsiae must enter host cells in order to grow and survive. They have evolved many mechanisms to use the patient's endothelial cells to their advantage. To enter a cell, the rickettsia must attach to a molecule on the surface of the cell. *Rickettsia rickettsii* has at least two proteins on the outside of its bacterial cell wall that adhere to the receptor proteins on the endothelial cell membrane. Receptor proteins usually bind to molecules such as hormones that control normal cell activity. One of the receptors to which rickettsia binds is a host protein that serves diverse functions in the host nucleus, cytoplasm, and surface membrane. Rickettsiae evolved to take advantage of this cell protein for use as a receptor, a function unrelated to the host cell's use of the same protein.

The subsequent steps are further evidence of rickettsial exploitation of the host cells. **Binding** to the first receptor sends a message to the cell to send more receptors to bind the rickettsia securely and to engulf it. These events occur within minutes, and then the rickettsia is inside the cell, inside a pocket surrounded by the host membrane known as a phagosome. The rickettsia next produces enzymes that digest the membrane, allowing the rickettsia to escape from the phagosome into the cytosol of the host cell. There the rickettsia can use its special transporter mechanisms to steal the materials from the host cell that it needs to grow.

### SPREAD OF *RICKETTSIA RICKETTSII* BETWEEN CELLS

Some bacteria have genes that encode the proteins for **flagella**, organelles on the outer surface of the cell that allow bacteria to move from place to place by a coordinated waving motion. The result is an effect like swimming. Rickettsiae have no flagellar genes. They travel through the body by another means. They secrete a protein onto their surface that activates **polymerization** of bundles of a host cell protein called **actin**. Polymerization is a process by which many smaller molecules are joined together to form a larger molecule. In this case, small round molecules of actin are joined into long filaments. The continuous formation of bundles of these filaments on one end of the rickettsia pushes the bacterium forward in the host cell cytoplasm. Some rickettsiae propelled in this way collide with the host cell membrane and deform it outwards and into the neighboring cell. The stretched host cell membrane breaks, perhaps by an as yet undiscovered rickettsial activity, and the rickettsia finds itself in a fresh healthy cell with plenty more nutrients for further growth. Some of the rickettsiae break through the host cell membrane into the bloodstream and spread to a new location to begin again the processes of attachment, engulfment, escape into the cytosol, and cell-to-cell spread.

## DEATH OF INFECTED ENDOTHELIAL CELLS

Rickettsial infection of endothelial cells triggers two sequences, one leading to cell death and the other directed toward preventing cell death. There are two main types of cell death, called **necrosis** and **apoptosis**. Necrosis can result from various kinds of severe injury; for example, dissolving the host cell membrane causing the cytoplasm and nucleus to leak out. It is caused by external damage to the cell. In contrast, apoptosis is death of the cell according to a programmed series of events that are executed by the cell itself, to remove it quickly and without causing any subsequent damaging effects.

Infection by *Rickettsia rickettsii* leads to inhibition of apoptosis. This impairment of programmed death of the infected cell benefits the intracellular bacteria. Because the rickettsiae must be inside a host cell to grow, keeping the cell alive maintains an intracellular home for the bacteria. Despite this, the endothelial cell may die anyway after further rickettsial growth and spread either via necrosis or apoptosis induced by other mechanisms. Infection of endothelial cells with *Rickettsia rickettsii* causes the endothelial cells to produce highly reactive forms of oxygen that damage the endothelial cell membranes. If the damage to the cell membranes is too severe, the endothelial cells undergo necrosis.

## INJURED ENDOTHELIUM CAUSES BLOOD VESSELS TO LEAK

The main consequence of rickettsial damage to the endothelial lining of blood vessels is increased leakiness of fluid from blood plasma into the surrounding tissues. The accumulation of fluid in tissue leads to swelling known as edema. The loss of fluid from the blood reduces the blood volume, and the blood pressure falls below normal. The heart does not pump as much blood to some organs as it normally would. Reduced blood flow to the kidneys results in impaired clearance of waste products from the body, a reversible form of acute renal failure. If the blood pressure falls too much, the

patient develops shock, and a more severe type of acute renal failure occurs.

The accumulation of edema in the arms and legs is not a serious condition, but when the lungs fill up with edema fluid that prevents oxygen from entering the air spaces of the lungs, a life-threatening condition exists. Similarly, rickettsial encephalitis with edema in the brain can result in coma, seizures, and death.

## WHY IS ESCHAR RARE IN ROCKY MOUNTAIN SPOTTED FEVER?

An eschar is composed of a thick black scab and the underlying damaged skin where a tick injected some other spotted fever group rickettsia. The word is derived from a Greek word meaning a hearth, or where burning occurs. An eschar looks like a small round mark left by a branding iron. It occurs in approximately 1 in 100 cases of Rocky Mountain spotted fever, but in the majority of infections caused by *R. akari*, *R. africae*, *R. conorii*, *R. honei*, *R. sibirica*, *R. slovaca*, and *R. australis*. The eschar results from extensive damage to an approximately 1-centimeter diameter network of infected blood vessels in the skin. *Rickettsia rickettsii* spreads to the brain and lungs, and does more damage in these vital organs, but the less virulent rickettsial species appear to remain at the tick bite site longer and do more damage to a small patch of skin there. Are these bacteria more adept at spreading from cell to neighboring cell? Is *Rickettsia rickettsii* more effective in invading the bloodstream and infecting distant organs? No one knows.

Less severe rickettsial infections are characterized by prominently enlarged lymph nodes that receive the draining lymph from the region of the eschar and by less extensive rash than is associated with Rocky Mountain spotted fever or even no rash at all. The name of the disease in Europe that is caused by *Rickettsia slovaca* is tick-borne lymphadenopathy, the medical name for enlarged lymph nodes. These patients

## HEMORRHAGE AND CLOTTING: A DELICATE BALANCE

The spots, or pinhead-sized hemorrhages in the center of the rash that give Rocky Mountain spotted fever its name, are caused by such severe injury to the endothelial lining of the blood vessels that not only fluid, but also red blood cells, escape the vessels. Similar tiny hemorrhages occur throughout

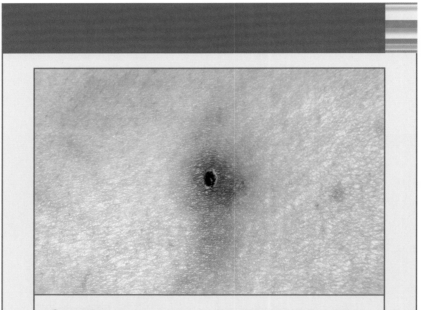

**Figure 5.1**   Close-up of an eschar at the bite point. (ISM/PhototakeUSA.com)

typically have neither fever nor rash, and the illness is not life-threatening. It is as if the spread of the infection beyond the eschar and nearby lymph node is minimal. Is this containment a characteristic of the bacteria or the result of effective patient's defenses? No one knows, but the answer, when finally found, will likely shed new light on the nature of Rocky Mountain spotted fever and rickettsial diseases in general.

the organs of the body, but life-threatening hemorrhage seldom occurs. Blood clots, plugs of **platelets** and **fibrin**, stop the loss of blood from areas of the vessels where the endothelial cells have died, detached, and been swept away in the flow of blood. The widespread infection of endothelial cells creates a state in which widespread coagulation of the blood can occur. If uncontrolled coagulation blocked the flow of blood, severe damage would be caused by interruption of the delivery of oxygen and nutrients. This disaster is averted by the balance of factors favoring clotting and those inhibiting clotting. In patients with Rocky Mountain spotted fever, blood clots occur where they are needed most, blood vessels are seldom blocked by clots, and rampant coagulation does not occur where it is not needed. Platelets being used to plug blood vessels causes

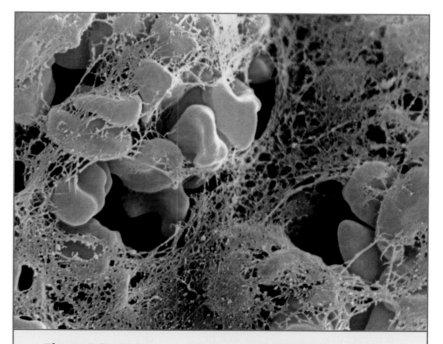

**Figure 5.2**    A blood clot, showing red blood cells trapped in fibrin. (Dr. David Phillips/Visuals Unlimited)

## TYPHUS, A CLOUDY STATE OF MIND

Many diseases caused by different species of *Rickettsia* have typhus in their names; for example, epidemic typhus, murine typhus, North Asian tick typhus, and Queensland tick typhus. The word "typhus" is derived from another Greek word, *typhos*, which means "smoky." This describes the altered mental state that occurs, particularly in the more severe rickettsial infections such as those caused by *Rickettsia rickettsii*, *R. prowazekii*, *R. conorii*, and *R. typhi*.

As in other organs, rickettsiae infect endothelial cells lining the blood vessels of the brain and cause inflammation of the brain, a condition known as encephalitis. Low blood pressure results in less blood being pumped to the brain, and if the lungs' function is also impaired, there is less oxygen in the blood that flows to the brain. All of these factors—edema, reduced blood flow, and low oxygen concentration in the blood—can cause confusion, delirium, and even coma.

a decrease in their concentration in the blood, but not below levels necessary to prevent bleeding.

## SYMPTOMS RELATED TO IMMUNE RESPONSE

The cells of the immune system secrete special proteins known as **cytokines**. These cytokines act locally on other cells to enhance the host's immune response and sometimes enter the blood and travel to a distant location to act. The names of several of the cytokines that are produced early in the disease are **interleukin-1**, **interleukin-6**, and **tumor necrosis factor**. The effects of these cytokines include setting the thermostat in the **hypothalamus** of the brain to a higher level, resulting in fever. Headache and muscle aches are also caused by the cytokines. Cytokines also play a role in killing rickettsiae and recovery from the illness, the subject of the next chapter.

# 6

# How the Immune System Fights Rickettsiae

The immune system is like an orchestra with many players and instruments that can function together to play the different musical pieces on the program. Rickettsial infection stimulates many of the different components of the immune system into action. When they work together promptly and efficiently, the patient clears the bacteria from the body and recovers from Rocky Mountain spotted fever.

## THE FIRST LINE OF DEFENSE

Immunologists, scientists who investigate the immune system, divide the immune response into two components: innate immunity and acquired immunity. Innate immunity occurs rapidly during the host's early encounter with an infectious agent. It follows a stereotyped script, responding in a similar way no matter what type of bacterium, virus, fungus, or parasite has attacked. There is no time to craft a special defense. Innate immunity is the first line of defense. Neutrophilic polymorphonuclear **leukocytes** are in this first line of defenders. They are the white blood cells that form pus as they rush into sites where bacteria that live outside of cells have invaded. They engulf these bacteria and try to prevent their spread. There is no evidence that they play a significant role in counterattacking rickettsiae, which sequester themselves inside host cells away from the reach of neutrophil leukocytes.

Another group of players on the innate immunity team are **natural killer cells**. Rickettsiae activate natural killer cells, which inhibit the growth of rickettsiae by secreting a host defense substance, **gamma interferon**. Gamma interferon is produced by several types of cells of

48

the immune system, particularly later during development of acquired immunity. Gamma interferon is a cytokine, a regulatory protein produced during the immune response. The rapid production of gamma interferon by natural killer cells dampens the rickettsial infection. All the *Rickettsia rickettsii* are not killed, but their numbers are smaller than if their growth was unchecked.

The potentially beneficial effects of other cytokines, such as **alpha interferon**, tumor necrosis factor, interleukin-6, and some cytokines produced by rickettsia-infected endothelial cells, are as yet undetermined. If, as is suspected, dendritic cells are an important early site of rickettsial infection in the skin and draining lymph node, the cytokines that they produce probably influence the direction that both innate and acquired immunity will take. For example, whether the dendritic cells produce interleukin-12 or alternatively interleukin-4 determines whether the response will be effective against intracellular bacteria or not. These cytokines are messengers that also communicate between cells of innate immunity and influence their responses in ways that favor destroying particular microbial invaders or not.

## THE SPECIFIC ADAPTIVE IMMUNE RESPONSE TO RICKETTSIAE

Acquired immunity takes several days to develop. Acquired immunity is the immune response directed against a new invader that the body has never seen before. It must attack specific components of the microbe. The immune system must select cells with receptors that bind to specific parts of rickettsial molecules and cells that produce antibodies to key rickettsial components. Then these cells must reproduce themselves to large numbers. The cells that combat the rickettsiae must travel to the locations of the infection, recognize the location, and enter the tissue there. The antibody-producing cells must manufacture and secrete enough antibodies to reach effective concentrations at the site of infection.

## THE ENDOTHELIAL CELL TURNS THE TABLES

If effectively activated by certain cytokines, endothelial cells can kill the rickettsiae growing inside them. The cytokines that activate human endothelial cells include gamma interferon and tumor necrosis factor, as well as, an important chemokine, known as **RANTES**, an acronym for "regulated on activation normal T expressed and secreted." Endothelial cells activated by these cytokines produce highly toxic, unstable nitric oxide and reactive oxygen containing molecules that attack rickettsiae, resulting in death of the bacteria. Cytokines also stimulate the production of an enzyme inside the cell that destroys **tryptophan**, an amino acid that rickettsiae need in order to grow and survive. These anti-rickettsial effects lead to an event called **autophagy** that was first discovered to be a host defense against intracellular bacteria in studies of rickettsiae. Autophagy is a process occurring inside the cell that has an end result like **phagocytosis**. In phagocytosis, the cell extends its surface cell membrane around a particle outside of the cell and pulls it inside into the cytoplasm surrounded by the host cell membrane. Autophagy entails the wrapping of a membrane around a particle *inside* the host cell's cytoplasm. Autophagy had been described previously as a means of disposing of worn out cellular organelles such as mitochondria. Both phagosomes (the structures containing formerly extracellular particles that were engulfed) and autophagosomes (the result of autophagy) fuse with **lysosomes** (membrane-surrounded spheres containing a mixture of substances including enzymes that can kill and digest organisms). Rickettsiae avoid the fate of destruction inside phagosomes after entry into cells by phagosomal escape as described in the previous chapter. Injured rickettsiae, however—harmed by nitric oxide, toxic oxygen-containing molecules, and tryptophan starvation— are susceptible to autophagy, exposure to lysosomal contents, death, and digestion by the enzymes.

## THE SOURCE OF CYTOKINES THAT
## ACTIVATE ENDOTHELIAL CELLS

When a pathologist looks in a microscope at a network of infected blood vessels in a small sample of skin taken early in the course of illness, the changes are subtle. In contrast, later in the illness, such a sample shows a prominent population of immune cells that crawled through the layer of endothelial cells and accumulated around the infected blood vessel. These immune cells are the source of the cytokines that activate the adjacent endothelial cells to kill the intracellular rickettsiae. They are a mixture of lymphocytes and macrophages. The precise signals that enable them to recognize and enter the infected region have not been identified. Science never runs out of unanswered questions.

## THE CRITICAL TYPE OF LYMPHOCYTE
## FOR RECOVERY

Lymphocytes, another kind of white blood cell, are classified by their functions and by the different proteins that they have on their cell membrane. Some lymphocytes, called B cells, are destined to mature into antibody-producing cells. Other lymphocytes are called T cells. Two of the membrane proteins on distinct populations of T cells are called CD4 and CD8. Both CD4 and CD8 T lymphocytes secrete cytokines such as gamma interferon that, as described above, activate rickettsial killing mechanisms. CD8 T lymphocytes, however, have another important function that is required to eliminate the rickettsial infection. Cytotoxic CD8 T lymphocytes bind to rickettsial proteins presented on special structures of the surface of infected cells. This binding triggers cytotoxic events, including the injection of a substance called **perforin** and the initiation of a series of signals that leads to programmed cell death of the infected cell. The rickettsia-induced anti-apoptotic state is overcome. Apoptosis of the remaining infected endothelial cells removes the last rickettsiae. Without cytotoxic CD8 T

lymphocytes, the infection will result in death or persistence of the rickettsiae.

## ANTIBODIES AND RICKETTSIAL INFECTION

It did not seem logical that antibodies would influence a rickettsial infection because rickettsiae were inside cells and antibodies were in the fluids outside the cells. What a surprise when experiments showed that if animals were given antibodies to the rickettsiae before rickettsial infection, they were protected. Further experiments showed that if the antibodies were transfused early enough in the course of illness, they could save the life of an experimentally infected mouse.

## TYPHUS AND WAR

Epidemic louse-borne typhus was a major factor affecting the history of Europe from the early 1500s until the mid-1900s. The outcome of many wars was determined by which army was infected first with *Rickettsia prowazekii*. Lack of opportunities to bathe and wash clothes led to a high prevalence of body louse infestation among soldiers and displaced civilians. The invasion of Russia by Napoleon's Grand Army in 1812 was stopped neither by the Russian Army nor the bitter cold weather but by a horrible epidemic of typhus. At the end of World War I and during the Russian Revolution, 30 million cases of typhus occurred in Russia with 3 million deaths. As recently as the civil war in Burundi in the mid-1990s, there were 100,000 cases of louse-borne typhus. Thus, it is remarkable that during World War II, when epidemics of typhus raged among the civilian population of North Africa and the Middle East, no American soldier died of louse-borne typhus. The reason is that all had received a protective vaccine. Although the vaccine was not perfect and was later removed from the market, it made the difference. Soldiers still got typhus, but they didn't die.

The cell wall of *Rickettsia rickettsii* contains three major components: outer membrane protein A, outer membrane protein B, and lipopolysaccharide. Transfused antibodies to either outer membrane protein A or B protected against disease, but antibodies to lipopolysaccharide did not. Antibodies against rickettsial outer membrane protein B prevented rickettsiae from escaping the phagosome. Trapped inside the phagosome, the rickettsiae were killed and digested by the contents of lysosomes that were dumped into the phagosome.

Early in the course of the experimental infection, mice produced antibodies to lipopolysaccharide. The infected

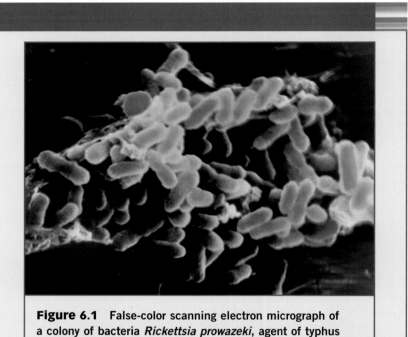

**Figure 6.1** False-color scanning electron micrograph of a colony of bacteria *Rickettsia prowazeki*, agent of typhus disease. They cause epidemic typhus, a human disease transmitted by the human body louse. (CNRI/Photo Researchers, Inc.)

mice, however, did not produce antibodies against the outer membrane proteins that were important for protection until too late in the infection to alter the outcome of an experimental

## ARCHAIC SCIENCE GETS THE RIGHT ANSWER

The purpose of the typhus vaccine was to prevent disease upon later exposure to *Rickettsia prowazekii*, a situation similar to re-infection. The Food and Drug Administration (FDA) has particular tests of potency that are required before a production batch of vaccine that has been manufactured can be sold. In the 1970s, the test to assess the potency of the typhus vaccine was based on observing the effect produced in mice by antibodies from vaccinated guinea pigs. The antibody test was cumbersome and convoluted. The immunized guinea pig's serum had to be evaluated to determine its ability to prevent a toxic death of mice injected with a high dose of typhus rickettsiae. Determining the effective dilution was a quantitative measure. Several aspects of the potency assay for the typhus vaccine seemed inappropriate. It was not based on preventing infection in the mice, which are not even susceptible to infection with *Rickettsia prowazekii*.

Why did the toxicity assessment of the vaccine accurately predict its protective capacity? We now know that the toxicity test depends on antibody reactivity with particular parts of the rickettsial outer surface that were unknown in the 1970s. These are the targets of antibodies that prevent reinfection. Although it was not fully understood at the time, the vaccine prevented soldiers from dying. The method served its practical purpose effectively in a period when less was known about immunology and rickettsiae.

lethal challenge dose. Thus, naturally produced antibodies could prevent *re*-infection but likely did not play a significant role in recovery from a primary infection.

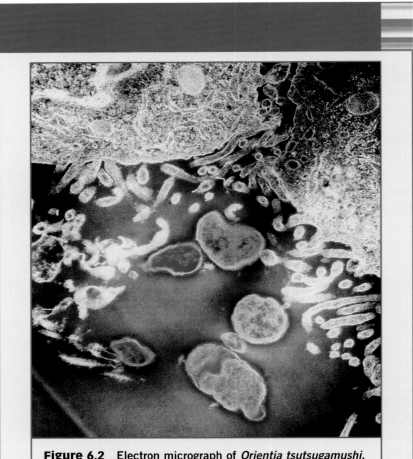

**Figure 6.2**  Electron micrograph of *Orientia tsutsugamushi*, gram-negative rickettsial microorganisms, shown inside the peritoneal cavity of an infected mouse. (Scott Camazine/ Phototake)

# 7
# How to Make a Diagnosis

When Rocky Mountain spotted fever was first seen in the Rocky Mountain region of Montana and Idaho, some doctors knew that it resembled another disease that was later shown to be caused by a rickettsia, namely typhus fever. Others called it black measles and other names. Soon, they came to expect cases to appear in the late spring and new cases to disappear by mid-summer. They recognized its clinical features such as the hemorrhagic-spotted rash and the high lethality. They made the diagnosis on the basis of the epidemiology (when and where cases occurred) and the clinical manifestations.

## DIAGNOSIS BY ISOLATION OF *RICKETTSIA RICKETTSII*

Howard T. Ricketts, an assistant professor of pathology at the University of Chicago, arrived in western Montana in 1906 to study the disease. Adult male guinea pigs that he inoculated with blood taken from patients with Rocky Mountain spotted fever developed fever and swelling and hemorrhages in the skin of the scrotum. This consistent observation served as the first objective diagnostic test for Rocky Mountain spotted fever. It was based on spread of the as-yet-to-be-discovered *Rickettsia rickettsii* through the bloodstream to the blood vessels of the scrotum, where they grew particularly well because the cooler temperature in this external surface was more favorable to the rickettsiae than the high temperature of the guinea pigs' internal organs.

Isolation of these bacteria that grew only inside cells could not be accomplished by inoculating Petri dishes containing agar or test tubes containing nutrient broth. More than 30 years later, it was discovered

that rickettsiae could be isolated in embryonated chicken eggs. Hospital laboratories, however, did not maintain guinea pigs or supplies of embryonated eggs. Even today, when cell culture is routinely used in university hospitals to isolate viruses, the clinical microbiology laboratories do not attempt to diagnose Rocky Mountain spotted fever by isolating rickettsiae because these dangerous organisms require a biosafety level 3 laboratory, as described previously.

## DIAGNOSIS BY DETECTING ANTIBODIES

In 1909, W.J. Wilson from Belfast, Ireland, reported isolating a **bacillus** from stools and urine of typhus patients. He showed that the sera of typhus patients caused these bacteria to clump together, called **agglutination**. In 1916, in Berlin, E. Weil and A. Felix obtained similar results with an isolate of *Proteus vulgaris* bacteria from patients' urine. These bacteria were not the cause of typhus, but they contained molecules that reacted with antibodies to *Rickettsia prowazekii*. A much-needed diagnostic test for typhus was developed and has been known as the Weil-Felix test ever since. By today's standards, the test is far from ideal. The serum of some patients who do not have a rickettsial infection still contains antibodies that react with these bacteria, causing false-positive agglutination. Also, many patients with rickettsial infections fail to agglutinate either of the two strains of *Proteus vulgaris*, namely OX-19 and OX-2, giving false negative results. In some locations in developing countries, however, the choice is between *Proteus* agglutination testing or no test at all. Indeed, this poor method still yields useful information, including the first clues leading to the identification of the agents of the emerging infectious diseases Japanese spotted fever (*Rickettsia japonica*) and Flinders Island spotted fever (*Rickettsia honei*). Currently, more accurate tests for antibodies to *Rickettsia rickettsii* employ the actual organisms or their components to test for diagnostic antibodies.

The testing of sera for the presence of antibodies is called serology. The gold-standard test (against which the performance of new tests must be compared) for Rocky Mountain spotted fever is the immunofluorescent antibody assay, known widely as IFA. The IFA uses cells containing the whole organisms of *Rickettsia rickettsii.* Thus, every component of the rickettsia is available for reaction with antibodies in the patient's serum. The rickettsia-infected cells are placed in wells on a microscope slide and immersed in acetone that dissolves holes in the host cell membrane, allowing antibodies to enter the cell and bind to the rickettsiae. Dilutions of the patient's serum are made starting at 1 part serum to 64 parts physiologic salt solution and on upwards with increasing amounts of solution. These dilutions are placed on the rickettsia-containing wells and incubated under conditions that allow binding. Unbound antibodies are washed away, and the slide is incubated with a second antibody that is directed against human antibody molecules. This second anti-human antibody is connected to a fluorescent molecule that emits light when exposed to a particular wavelength of ultraviolet light. If human antibodies have bound to the rickettsiae, the fluorescent anti-human antibodies bind to them. After washing again, the slide is examined in a fluorescent microscope. If serum antibodies have attached to the rickettsiae, the organisms will glow bright green because of the fluorescent label on the second antibody.

When a person has Rocky Mountain spotted fever, they usually go to a doctor on the second or third day of illness. If a serologic test is performed at this time, no antibody to *Rickettsia rickettsii* will be detected. Indeed, a low concentration of antibodies, often only at 1-to-64 dilution, does not usually appear until day 7 or later. Laboratory confirmation of the diagnosis requires that a second serum sample be examined by IFA after the patient has clinically recovered. For the diagnosis to be confirmed, the second sample must react with a dilution of serum at least a four-fold greater than the

**Figure 7.1**   S. Burt Wolbach.  (U.S. National Library of Medicine)

first sample, e.g., first serum at 1 to 64 and second serum at 1 to 256. Thus serologic diagnoses are generally retrospective, confirmed only after the patient has recovered.

## DIAGNOSIS BY SEEING THE RICKETTSIAE IN TISSUE

Between 1916 and 1919, S. Burt Wolbach, a pathologist at Harvard University, developed a method for staining

*Rickettsia rickettsii* in infected tissues of fatal human cases of Rocky Mountain spotted fever and of experimentally infected guinea pigs. Seeing the small bacillary bacteria in endothelial cells established the diagnosis of rickettsial infection.

During the mid-1970s, the author of this book and the late Dr. Theodore Woodard independently used this approach to establish the diagnosis of Rocky Mountain spotted fever in living patients. They took a small skin biopsy obtained with a cutting punch that cored a 3-millimeter-diameter sample of anesthetized skin at the site of one of the rash spots. The sample was taken immediately to the laboratory and frozen. Thin, frozen slices were cut with a special machine, a frozen section microtome. The slices were incubated with antibodies to *Rickettsia rickettsii* that were labeled with fluorescein. After washing and searching the tissue on a fluorescent microscope, the presence of brightly glowing small bacillary bacteria in the cells lining blood vessels established the diagnosis. The patient's doctor was notified immediately that the diagnosis was Rocky Mountain spotted fever. In terms of guiding appropriate treatment, this approach is more effective than detecting antibodies, which would not yet be present. Currently, there are newer methods that can be applied to tissues that are fixed in formaldehyde and embedded in paraffin. The rickettsiae are stained with dyes that are visible in an ordinary light microscope. Unfortunately, few hospitals offer this diagnostic test, mainly because the number of rickettsia cases at any one hospital are very small.

## DIAGNOSIS BY DETECTING A TINY AMOUNT OF RICKETTSIAL DNA

A method called polymerase chain reaction, or PCR, uses an enzyme that amplifies the DNA of a specific gene millions of times. Thus, the DNA of a few bacteria containing a few copies of the gene can be increased from a level that is below the limit

of detection to a readily detectable amount. This approach has been applied to detection and identification of rickettsiae. The key is obtaining a sample that contains rickettsiae for PCR amplification. Infected ticks and organ samples of infected persons are samples in which rickettsiae are readily detected, but unfortunately, early in the course of Rocky Mountain spotted fever when a diagnosis is needed, there is a very low concentration of rickettsiae in the patient's blood. Most of the rickettsiae are in endothelial cells attached to the wall of the blood vessel. Thus, PCR of blood often yields negative results, i.e., no rickettsiae detected, until late in the disease when rickettsiae are released in large quantities into the blood and endothelial cells detach and also circulate.

## A LIFE-SAVING DECEPTION BASED ON THE WEIL-FELIX TEST

In Poland during World War II, it was dangerous to be Jewish, a gypsy, or anyone whom the Nazis wanted to destroy. A physician managed to steer the Nazis away from some villages where people were hiding. He was required to send sera from persons who might have epidemic louse-borne typhus fever to the central authorities for testing. Regions where typhus was active were avoided by the Germans. There was no treatment for typhus, and many infected persons died. The Nazis did not want to be exposed to typhus.

The local doctor prepared an inoculum of killed *Proteus* bacteria that would not cause an infection but would stimulate antibodies that would agglutinate *Proteus vulgaris* OX-19 in the Weil-Felix test. He injected it into the villagers. By sending sera from people injected with his material, he scared away the Germans and protected the inhabitants of his region. The invading authorities were convinced that typhus was rampant there.

## IN THE ABSENCE OF A DIAGNOSTIC TEST

A doctor who suspects the diagnosis of Rocky Mountain spotted fever based on the time of year (tick season), geographic region, potential tick exposure, and clinical signs and symptoms consistent with Rocky Mountain spotted fever, but does not have access to a means of laboratory diagnosis, will usually treat the patient with an antirickettsial antibiotic just to be on the safe side. The physician will not rely upon detecting antibodies early in the illness, but will rely on epidemiologic and clinical knowledge.

# 8

# How an Effective Antibiotic Works Against Rickettsiae

The principle of **antimicrobial** therapy is to administer a medicine that harms the **microbial** agent but not the patient. Some of the earliest antimicrobial drugs contained heavy metals such as arsenic, bismuth, or antimony that were only somewhat less poisonous to the patient than to the infectious agent.

The ideal antimicrobial drug kills the infecting organism. They are called **bactericidal** drugs. There are no antibiotics that kill rickettsiae. In fact, there are only two antimicrobial drugs that improve the outcome of patients with Rocky Mountain spotted fever, namely tetracycline and chloramphenicol. Both of these act by inhibiting rickettsial protein synthesis at the level of the bacterial **ribosome**. Unable to synthesize new protein, *Rickettsia rickettsii* cannot grow. These drugs' ability to stop the growth of rickettsiae is described as **bacteriostatic** or **rickettsiostatic**. Thus, their beneficial effect is inhibiting the progression of the disease so the immune system has time to generate a bactericidal attack.

## DETERMINANTS OF ANTIMICROBIAL USEFULNESS

Some bacteria have genes encoded in their chromosomes that can destroy the antibiotic. Penicillins are a class of drugs known as **beta-lactams** because of their chemical structure. Rickettsiae have the genetic ability to block the activity of beta-lactam drugs, which are ineffective in treating Rocky Mountain spotted fever. Another condition that must be met is

that the drug must be distributed to the site where the bacteria reside and be active under the conditions there, such as acidity. Rickettsiae reside in the cytosol of endothelial cells. Some antibiotics, such as gentamicin do not enter cells. Thus, gentamicin and other drugs restricted to the extracellular space are not effective against rickettsiae.

Each combination of bacterium and antibiotic has a concentration of the drug at which the bacteria are killed (minimal bactericidal concentration) or are inhibited from growth (minimal bacteriostatic concentration). For *Rickettsia rickettsii*, the important concentration would be that in the cytoplasm of endothelial cells. If the dose of tetracycline or chloramphenicol is too low, the rickettsial growth will not be inhibited and the disease will progress. Conversely, if the dose is too high, the patient will suffer the toxic effects of the drug. Because children are smaller, their dose of tetracycline or chloramphenicol must be calculated according to their body weight to avoid too high or too low a concentration. Children younger than eight years of age are still forming their permanent teeth, and tetracycline may cause permanent discoloration of these teeth. Fortunately, doxycycline, a very effective drug of the tetracycline class, does not stain the teeth and is the preferred drug not only for adults but also for young children.

## CHOICE OF ANTIBIOTICS

No one has ever done a prospective controlled comparison of different drugs for the treatment of Rocky Mountain spotted fever. It has been observed that many drugs used to treat patients are ineffective, and that patients do not improve and indeed may die. Studies of cell cultures infected with *Rickettsia rickettsii* and treated with these antibiotics confirm that these drugs are ineffective at doses that can be achieved safely.

Studies comparing the outcomes of patients with Rocky Mountain spotted fever who were treated with a tetracycline or with chloramphenicol are hard to interpret. Risk factors for more severe illness, such as age and duration of illness before

beginning treatment, must be the same in both groups of treated patients. If one group contains more elderly patients, it would be expected to have a higher rate of fatalities. If one group began its treatment later, a higher occurrence of death would be expected. After these and other factors were accounted for, it was determined by the Centers for Disease Control and Prevention that doxycycline was more effective than chloramphenicol in preventing death from Rocky Mountain spotted fever.

Patients with Mediterranean spotted fever caused by *Rickettsia conorii* are usually not as severely ill as patients with Rocky Mountain spotted fever. Fluoroquinolone antimicrobials have been used to treat Mediterranean spotted fever patients successfully. Children with mild cases of Mediterranean spotted fever have even been treated effectively with azithromycin and

## KEEPING THE PATIENT'S CONDITION STABLE

There is more to treating a deadly disease like Rocky Mountain spotted fever than inhibiting bacterial growth. The patient's blood volume must be maintained by giving the right amount of intravenous fluids. Complications must be managed. For example, if seizures occur, anticonvulsant drugs must be given. Nursing care is very important. Often patients must be admitted to an intensive care unit. Mechanical ventilation and supplemental oxygen may be required to correct a low oxygen concentration in the blood caused by respiratory failure. Cardiac monitoring may be needed if abnormal heart rhythm occurs. When acute renal failure is not corrected by replenishment of blood volume and restored blood flow to the kidneys, some patients must be placed on an artificial kidney dialysis machine. Some patients' survival follows a rocky road, and their condition must be carefully stabilized to allow antibiotics and their immune system to work.

clarithromycin. None of these antimicrobial agents has been shown to be effective for treating Rocky Mountain spotted fever, and their use is not recommended.

As strange as it might seem, there is one class of antimicrobial drugs, namely the sulfonamides, that makes the disease even worse than if it were not treated at all.

## DURATION OF TREATMENT

Of course, no one will ever do a study to see how short a course of doxycycline can be given to achieve a favorable outcome. It would be unethical. Some patients would be harmed because they would not be treated long enough, and their immune system would not have cleared the rickettsiae. The signs and symptoms of the illness would reappear. Thus, when a patient's fever and other symptoms disappear, treatment should be continued for 48 to 72 hours more in order to avoid a relapse.

# 9

# Avoiding Rocky Mountain Spotted Fever

The key to avoiding Rocky Mountain spotted fever is preventing ticks from injecting rickettsiae into one's skin. Staying indoors from May until the end of September to keep from being exposed to ticks would be an unnecessary precaution. When walking in areas where ticks abound, however, such as the high grass along the side of a trail, along a roadside, on the bank of a stream, or in a vacant lot or uncultivated field, it is wise to wear protective clothing. Long pants tucked into one's socks prevent ticks from attaching to the skin. Long sleeves prevent ticks that have climbed to the top of a long blade of tall grasses from grasping the skin of one's passing arm with their outstretched legs.

Some experts recommend wearing light colored pants. The presence of a dark tick is most visible on white pants. Once seen, the tick can be brushed off. An unseen tick can crawl to an opening to the skin even at the collar.

Treatment of the skin with a tick repellent such as DEET provides further protection. Treatment of clothing with a tick repellent such as permethrin can also be highly effective.

## HOW TO REMOVE A TICK THAT HAS ATTACHED TO THE SKIN

When a tick has attached, inserted its mouth parts into the skin, and begun to feed, prompt removal before it has injected any organisms can prevent infection with *Rickettsia rickettsii*. Although ticks have injected rickettsiae in as short a period as six hours after attachment, organisms are often not inoculated until 24 hours after attachment. Thus, checking the entire body at the end of the day in the field and removal of all ticks will prevent most

**Figure 9.1**   A man applies a Deet repellent to his clothing in order to repel insects.   (James Gathany/Centers for Disease Control and Prevention)

cases of Rocky Mountain spotted fever. Parents should examine their children for ticks every evening during tick season. It is important to examine not only the easily visible skin but also the scalp, armpits, and groin. Sometimes an attached tick, particularly in a hairy region, can be felt more readily with the fingers than seen with the eyes.

The best method for removing an attached tick is to grasp it with tweezers flush with the skin and to exert firm steady traction until the entire tick, including its mouth parts, are pulled free, often with a tiny fragment of skin. If the body of the tick is grasped and pulled, the mouth parts may break off and remain in the skin, where it may form a **nidus** for infection or chronic inflammation. Using tweezers avoids contact of

the fingers with internal fluids of the tick, which may contain *Rickettsia rickettsii* and be accidentally rubbed into the eye or a skin wound and cause the rickettsial infection to enter the body. Of course, a tick can be removed in a similar fashion with fingers protected by tissue paper or washed thoroughly after tick removal.

Folk customs advocate numerous ineffective, even dangerous, methods for removing ticks. Trying to induce a tick to detach by burning it with a lit cigarette or match risks harm without additional benefit. Covering a tick with Vaseline, nail polish, or other substances to asphyxiate it and cause it to detach delays timely removal of the tick without any advantage.

## VACCINES AGAINST
## ROCKY MOUNTAIN SPOTTED FEVER

In the mid-1920s at the Rocky Mountain Laboratory in the Bitterroot Valley of western Montana, Drs. Roscoe Spencer and R.R. Parker developed the first vaccine against Rocky Mountain spotted fever. Unable to cultivate the bacteria, they used their tick host for the propagation of *Rickettsia rickettsii*. They infected guinea pigs with the rickettsiae and then placed Rocky Mountain wood ticks on the infected animals. The ticks sucked rickettsia-containing blood from the guinea pigs, and *Rickettsia rickettsii* invaded cells throughout the ticks and grew within the tick cells. The ticks served as Spencer and Parker's test tube for propagating large quantities of *Rickettsia rickettsii*. At the peak of infection, the infected ticks were ground up, and the rickettsiae were inactivated chemically. This incredible mixture of ticks, guinea pig blood, and rickettsiae was the vaccine.

The vaccine required an annual booster shot to remain effective, but the injection site became more and more angrily inflamed with each year's shot. It saved lives, however. In a situation where the fatality rate was as high at 90 percent, only

10 percent of vaccinated persons who became ill with Rocky Mountain spotted fever died. It was not a perfect record, but it was substantially better than nothing.

Subsequent vaccines were produced in embryonated eggs and cell culture. Neither were field tested. The yolk sac vaccine did not protect volunteers against infection with *Rickettsia rickettsii*. The cell-culture-grown vaccine provided only 25

## TAKING ANTIBIOTICS DOES NOT PREVENT ROCKY MOUNTAIN SPOTTED FEVER

Some infections can be prevented by taking antibiotics. Meningitis caused by the bacterium *Neisseria meningitidis*, also known as meningococcus, is one example. This organism sometimes causes epidemics associated with person-to-person spread of the bacteria through personal contact. If a student in a college dormitory develops meningococcal meningitis, contacts of the patient are offered preventive treatment with appropriate antibiotics.

Treatment of healthy persons who have a tick bite, however, is not recommended. Attempts to use tetracycline to prevent illness in guinea pigs infected with *Rickettsia rickettsii* failed. The animals were inoculated with *Rickettsia rickettsii* and immediately given tetracycline, but began falling ill several days after the course of antibiotics was completed. The antibiotic treatment had delayed the onset of illness, but tetracycline had only slowed the growth of the rickettsiae and had not killed them. The bacteria had not grown to a sufficient amount to stimulate the animal's immune system, which is the mechanism by which the organisms must be killed. The rickettsiae survived by waiting until the antibiotic treatment stopped and then began growing unchecked by the immune system. Illness was just as severe as what untreated guinea pigs suffered.

percent protection. Persons who have had Rocky Mountain spotted fever once are solidly immune to reinfection. A protective vaccine could be developed, but there are no commercial vaccines available currently, mainly due to the scientific challenges of creating one, the rigors of the approval process, and the relatively low demand for such a vaccine.

# 10

# Defense Against Bioterrorism

**Terrorism is a reality of the 21st century. Although many resources are** devoted to combatting terrorists' use of explosives, preparations should be made to cope with other methods of creating panic and fear. Given the long planning and preparation that al-Qaeda devoted to the unexpected airliner attacks on the World Trade Center and the Pentagon, it is plausible to consider that terrorists might one day learn to obtain and deploy biological weapons of terrorism.

Most knowledge of biological weapons is based upon what was developed by national biowarfare weapon programs in Russia, the United Kingdom, Japan, and the United States. In 1928, a secret decree by the Soviets ordered the development of *Rickettsia prowazekii* into a battlefield weapon. By the 1930s, typhus was the first biologic weapon produced by the Soviets. There were both liquid and powder versions for use as an aerosol. In the 1930s and early 1940s, the Japanese performed biologic weapon research, including human and field testing, in northeastern China. The program included development of typhus as a bioweapon.

In the United States in 1996, governmental concern for the danger of bioterrorism led to creation of a list of organisms, called Select Agents, that were deemed illegal to possess, do research on, transport, or ship to another laboratory except under prescribed conditions. Each person who possessed one or more of these agents, each laboratory that performed research with them, and any institution that shipped or received them, had to be registered by the Department of Justice and certified by the Centers for Disease Control and Prevention. *Rickettsia rickettsii* and

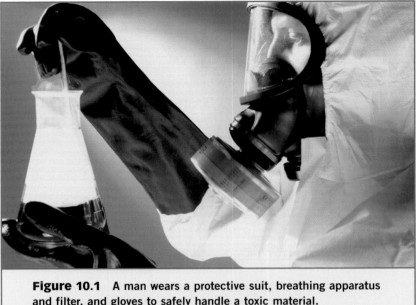

**Figure 10.1** A man wears a protective suit, breathing apparatus and filter, and gloves to safely handle a toxic material. (CC Studio/Photo Researchers, Inc.)

*Rickettsia prowazekii* are on the Select Agents list. The potential acquisition by terrorists is considered to be so dangerous that only specially registered scientists and certified laboratories are permitted to have them.

In 1999, when the CDC developed a prioritized list of bioterrorism threats, not surprisingly, agents of diseases such as anthrax, smallpox, and Ebola virus were placed in Category A, the most dangerous category. Placement of *Rickettsia prowazekii* in Category B and *Rickettsia rickettsii* in Category C raises questions about the validity of their criteria and the weight assigned to each of them. The factors that should be given importance in the prioritizing of potential biologic agents of terror include severity of illness, stability of aerosol infectivity, infective dose by aerosol, effectiveness of treatment, availability of the agent, and feasibility of growing the agent.

Rocky Mountain spotted fever is as severe an infection as plague and **tularemia** and more severe than **Rift Valley fever** and **Lassa fever**, all in Category A. The bacteria are a thousand times more infectious by aerosol than anthrax spores. It is not necessary to break into a high security laboratory to steal samples of *Rickettsia rickettsii*. These bacteria are in ticks in nature and can be isolated, cultivated, and preserved in a stable infectious form by a person with modest microbiologic skills using easily obtainable materials and equipment.

Compared with other agents, relatively little research is being done to develop vaccines or diagnostic tests, both of which are needed to prepare for a bioterrorist attack. Because doxycycline and chloramphenicol are effective treatments, no one has worried about developing new therapies. Rickettsiae resistant to each of these antibiotics have been developed by laboratory selection, dangerous and unethical acts by contemporary standards, which proscribe creating an organism more dangerous than what is found in nature. A terrorist would have no ethical qualms about using that approach or genetic engineering to create *Rickettsia rickettsii* organisms that are resistant to all antibiotics, and it would not be a difficult challenge.

If *Rickettsia rickettsii* resistant to doxycycline and chloramphenicol were used as a weapon of bioterrorism, an alternative treatment would be needed. Infusion of particular antibodies is one potential approach. Antibodies to outer membrane proteins A and B of *Rickettsia rickettsii* would enhance the chances of recovery from Rocky Mountain spotted fever if given early enough. Other therapeutic targets could be identified and treatments developed that chemically block or immunologically inhibit virulence mechanisms of *Rickettsia rickettsii*.

The number of scientists investigating rickettsiae and rickettsial diseases is small. There are many bacteria and diseases that they cause. Scientists must learn many disciplines, including microbiology, immunology, medicine, pathology,

epidemiology, and entomology, to discover unknown facts. The need and opportunities for young scientists to enter the field of rickettsiology extends throughout the world from the

## WHAT IS BEING DONE TO PROTECT AGAINST A BIOTERRORIST ATTACK?

After the anthrax attacks through the U.S. Postal Service in 2001, the National Institutes of Health developed a strategy to prepare against microbial dissemination by terrorists. Congress appropriated money to support research to develop new treatments, vaccines, and diagnostic tests.

Many of the relevant diseases had been neglected by science. Indeed, few scientists do research on *Rickettsia rickettsii* or *Rickettsia prowazekii*, and there are at present few medical doctors who have devoted energy to the investigation of Rocky Mountain spotted fever or epidemic typhus. This challenge to our nation and the availability of funds to support research projects brought out the best efforts of many microbiologists, virologists, immunologists, and other biomedical scientists. Groups of experts selected the most useful projects for governmental support. The projects are currently making progress under careful evaluation. In contrast to the usual competitive efforts to be the one person who is the winner of the scientific race, these scientists are trying to assist one another in the successful development of novel drugs against untreatable viruses, of diagnostic tests that will rapidly identify what organism causes an attack so that appropriate treatment and preventive measures can be implemented, and of vaccines that can prevent the diseases. These efforts will improve the health of the world. It usually takes 10 years or longer, however, from the proof that a scientific principle is correct until it reaches the stage of production of the drug or vaccine and approval by the Food and Drug Administration that it is safe and effective and can be used.

research-intensive laboratories of universities to the clinics and field areas of the tropics. Rapidly advancing scientific methods are available to aid in research. Some adventurous members of the young generation would be most welcome to join the pursuit of new knowledge of rickettsiae.

# Glossary

**actin**—An intracellular protein found especially in microfilaments and active in muscular contraction, cellular movement, and maintenance of cell shape

**agar**—A gelatinous colloidal extract of algae used especially in culture media on which to grow bacteria in the lab

**agent**—Something that produces or is capable of producing an effect (e.g., bacteria are agents that cause infectious diseases)

**agglutination**—A reaction in which particles (as red blood cells or bacteria) suspended in a liquid collect into clumps (e.g., a serologic response to a specific antibody)

**alpha interferon**—A cytokine produced by various white blood cells that inhibits viral replication, suppresses cell proliferation, and regulates the immune response

**antimicrobial**—Destroying or inhibiting the growth of microorganisms and especially pathogenic microorganisms

**apoptosis**—A genetically determined process of cell self-destruction activated either by the presence of a stimulus or by the removal of a stimulus or suppressing agent; a normal physiological process eliminating DNA-damaged, superfluous, or unwanted cells (e.g., immune cells targeted against the self in the development of self-tolerance, or cells of a developmental stage of an embryo during the next stage of development); when halted, may result in uncontrolled cell growth and tumor formation

**arthropod**—A group of animals with a hard chitin-containing covering of their body (e.g., insects, ticks, and mites)

**autophagy**—The internal engulfment of a cellular part that is followed by its digestion by enzymes of the same cell

**bacillus**—A straight, rod-shaped microorganism

**bactericidal**—Kills bacteria

**bacteriostatic**—Causes inhibition or slowing of the growth of bacteria without destruction

**beta-lactams**—A group of antibiotics, such as penicillin, that prevent bacterial cell wall synthesis

**binding**—Combining or attaching to, especially a receptor to its ligand

**biosafety level 3 laboratory**—A microbiology laboratory designed with special protections to prevent infection of laboratory workers or escape of dangerous bacteria, such as rickettsiae, or viruses

# Glossary

**causative**—The cause of

**cytokine**—Any of a class of immunoregulatory proteins (such as interleukin, tumor necrosis factor, and interferon) that are secreted by cells especially of the immune system

**cytosol**—The fluid portion of the interior, or cytoplasm, of a cell, not including organelles and membranes

**dendritic cells**—A particular type of mononuclear phagocytic cell that ingests particles and processes them for the development of an immune response

**edema**—An abnormal accumulation of serous fluid in tissues or in a serous cavity

**endothelial cells or endothelium**—Thin, flat cells that line the blood vessels

**engorged**—Full to the limit of body capacity; e.g., a tick full of blood

**epidemiology**—A branch of medical science that deals with the incidence, distribution, and control of disease in a population

**eschar**—A thick scab and the underlying damaged tissue, formed especially after a burn

**fibrin**—The protein that forms a blood clot

**flagella**—A long tapering process that projects singly or in groups from a cell and is the primary organ of motion of many microorganisms

**gamma interferon**—A cytokine produced by T cells that regulates the immune response (as by the activation of macrophages) and is used in the control of infections

**Gram negative**—A type of bacterium that does not stain by Gram's method due to its cell wall composition

**Gram positive**—A type of bacteria that does stain by Gram's method due to its cell wall composition

**host**—A living animal or plant on or in which a parasite lives

**hypothalamus**—Basal part of the brain that includes vital regulatory centers

**immune**—Having a high degree of resistance to a disease

**incidence**—Rate of new cases of disease in a certain defined time period

**inoculate**—To introduce microorganisms into an animal or a culture medium

**interleukin-1**—A cytokine produced by lymphocytes, macrophages, and monocytes that functions especially in regulation of cell-mediated and humoral immune responses by activating lymphocytes and also mediates other biological processes (as the onset of fever), usually associated with infection and inflammation

**interleukin-6**—A cytokine that is produced by macrophages, fibroblasts, T cells, and tumor cells and that causes fever, induces maturation of B cells, activates and induces proliferation of T cells, and stimulates synthesis of plasma proteins (such as fibrinogen)

**Lassa fever**—A disease in west Africa that is caused by Lassa virus and is characterized by a high fever, headaches, mouth ulcers, muscle aches, small hemorrhages under the skin, heart and kidney failure, and a high mortality rate

**leukocytes**—Also known as white blood cells, they are colorless, lack hemoglobin, contain a nucleus, and include the lymphocytes, monocytes, neutrophils, eosinophils, and basophils

**lysosome**—A saclike cellular organelle that contains various hydrolytic enzymes

**macrophage**—A phagocytic tissue cell of the immune system that may be fixed or freely motile, that helps destroy foreign particles (as bacteria and viruses), and serves as an antigen-presenting cell

**macules**—Flat, colored skin lesions

**microbial**—Of, relating to, caused by, or being microbes

**mitochondria**—A round or long cellular organelle of most cells containing nuclei that is found in the cytoplasm and produces energy for the cell through cellular respiration

**molt**—To periodically shed an outer layer

**natural killer cells**—A lymphocyte of the innate immune system that can destroy target cells and produce particular cytokines

**necrosis**—Death of living tissue and cells

**nidus**—A place in tissue where organisms lodge and multiply

**obligate**—Biologically essential for survival

**organelles**—Specialized cellular parts (e.g., mitochondrion or ribosome)

**perforin**—A protein produced by cytotoxic T lymphocytes and natural killer cells that creates a hole in a target cell membrane

# Glossary

**phagocyte**—A cell (as a white blood cell) that engulfs and consumes foreign material (as microorganisms) and debris

**phagocytosis**—The engulfing of particulate matter that serves as an important bodily defense mechanism against infection by microorganisms and against contamination of mucosal surfaces or tissues by foreign particles and tissue debris

**platelets**—A minute, colorless a-nucleate disk-like cell of mammalian blood that assists in blood clotting by adhering to other platelets and to damaged endothelium

**polymerization**—A chemical reaction in which two or more small molecules combine to form larger molecules that contain repeating structural units of the original molecules

**RANTES**—A chemokine that causes lymphocytes to home in on a location

**repletion**—The act of eating to fullness

**ribosome**—Cytoplasmic granules that are sites of protein synthesis

**rickettsiostatic**—Inhibiting the growth of rickettsiae

**Rift Valley fever**—An acute, viral, mosquito-borne disease usually of domestic animals (such as sheep and cattle) in eastern and southern Africa that is marked by fever, spontaneous abortion, death of newborns, diarrhea, and jaundice in animals, and is sometimes transmitted to humans as a severe hemorrhagic fever

**satiated**—Satisfied

**transovarian transmission**—The maintenance of an infectious agent from one generation to the next via infection of the egg

**tryptophan**—An essential amino acid that is widely distributed in proteins

**tularemia**—An infectious disease especially of wild rabbits, rodents, humans, and some domestic animals that is caused by a bacterium (*Francisella tularensis*) and is transmitted especially by the bites of ticks and insects. In humans, it is marked by symptoms (as fever) of toxemia

**tumor necrosis factor**—A protein that is produced chiefly by monocytes and macrophages in response to endotoxins, that mediates inflammation, and that induces the activation of white blood cells

**vector**—A host that transmits an infectious agent to another host (e.g., a mosquito injecting yellow fever virus into a person)

# Bibliography

## Books

Aikawa, Jerry K. *Rocky Mountain Spotted Fever.* Springfield, Ill.: Charles C. Thomas Publisher, 1966.

Anderson, Burt, et al. *Rickettsial Infection and Immunity.* New York: Plenum Press, 1997.

Bouyer, Donald H., and David H. Walker. "*Rickettsia rickettsii* and other members of the spotted fever group as potential bioweapons." In *Microorganisms and Bioterrorism,* edited by B. Anderson, H. Friedman, and M. Bendinelli. New York: Springer, 2006.

Burgodorfer W., and R.L. Anacker, eds. *Rickettsiae and Rickettsial Diseases.* New York: Academic Press, 1981.

Harden, Victoria A. *Rocky Mountain Spotted Fever.* Baltimore and London: The Johns Hopkins University Press, 1997.

Hechemy, Karim E. *Rickettsiology Present and Future Directions.* New York: The New York Academy of Sciences, 2003.

Hechemy, Karim E., et al. *Rickettsioses From Genome to Proteome, Pathobiology, and Rickettsiae as an International Threat.* New York: The New York Academy of Sciences, 2005.

Philip, Robert N. *Rocky Mountain Spotted Fever in Western Montana.* Hamilton, Mont.: Bitter Root Valley Historical Society, 2000.

Raoult, Didier, and Philippe Brouqui. *Rickettsiae and Rickettsial Diseases at the Turn of the Third Millennium.* Paris: Elsevier, 1999.

Rehacek, Josef, and Irina V. Tarasevich. *Acari-borne Rickettsiae & Rickettsioses in Eurasia.* Bratislava, Russia: Veda Publishing House of the Slovak Academy of Sciences, 1988.

Sexton, D.J., and David H. Walker. "Spotted fever group rickettsioses." In *Tropical Infectious Diseases: Principles, Pathogens, and Practice, 2nd ed,* edited by R.L. Guerrant, D.H. Walker, and P.F. Weller. Philadelphia: Elsevier Churchill Livingstone, 2006.

Walker, David H. *Biology of Rickettsial Diseases.* Boca Raton, Fla.: CRC Press. 1988.

Walker, David H. "Rickettsial and Ehrlichial Infections." In *Conn's Current Therapy 2006,* edited by R.E. Rakel, and E.T. Bope. Philadelphia: Elsevier, 2006.

Walker, David H., and D. Sexton. "*Rickettsia rickettsii.*" In *Antimicrobial Therapy and Vaccines, 2nd ed.* New York: Apple Trees Productions, 2002.

# Bibliography

Walker, David H., and Didier Raoult. "*Rickettsia rickettsii* and other spotted fever group rickettsiae (Rocky Mountain spotted fever and other spotted fevers)." In *Principles and Practice of Infectious Diseases, 6th ed.,* edited by G.L. Mandell, J.E. Bennett, and R. Dolin. Philadelphia: Churchill Livingstone, 2004.

Walker, David H., and Donald H. Bouyer. "*Rickettsia.*" In *Manual of Clinical Microbiology, 8th ed.,* edited by P.R. Murray, et al. Washington, D.C.: ASM Press, 2003.

Wolbach, S.B., J.L. Todd, and F.W. Palfrey, eds. *The Etiology and Pathology of Typhus.* Cambridge, Mass.: League of Red Cross Societies at the Harvard University Press, 1922.

Zinsser, Hans. *Rats, Lice and History.* New York: Black Dog & Leventhal Publishers, 1963.

Yu, Xue-jie, and David H. Walker. "Family I. Rickettsiaceae." In *Bergey's Manual of Systematic Bacteriology, 2nd ed., vol. 2,* edited by D.J. Brenner, N.R. Kreig, and J.T. Staley. New York: Springer Science+Business Media, 2005.

## Articles

Billings, A.N., et al. "Rickettsial infection in murine models activates an early anti-rickettsial effect mediated by NK cells and associated with production of gamma interferon." *American Journal of Tropical Medicine and Hygiene* 65 (2001): 52–56.

Bozeman, F.M., et al. "Epidemic typhus rickettsiae isolated from flying squirrels." *Nature* 255 (1975): 545-547.

Breitschwerdt, E.B., et al. "Canine Rocky Mountain spotted fever: A kennel epizootic." *American Journal of Veterinary Research* 46 (1985): 2124–2128.

Burgdorfer, W. "Investigation of transovarial transmission of *Rickettsia rickettsii* in the wood tick, *Dermacentor andersonii.*" *Experimental Parasitology* 14 (1963): 152–159.

Burgdorfer, W., and D. Lackman. "Identification of *Rickettsia rickettsii* in the wood tick, *Dermacentor andersonii,* by means of fluorescent antibody." *Journal of Infectious Diseases* 107 (1960): 241–244.

Burgdorfer, W., K.T. Friedhoff, and J.L. Lancaster Jr. "Natural history of tickborne spotted fever in the USA: Susceptibility of small mammals to virulent *Rickettsia rickettsii.*" *Bull World Health Organization* 35 (1966):149–153.

Burgdorfer, W., V.F. Newhouse, E.G. Pickens, and D.B. Lackman. "Ecology of Rocky Mountain spotted fever in western Montana. Isolation of *Rickettsia*

*rickettsii* from wild mammals." *American Journal of Hygiene* 76 (1962): 293–301.

Chapman, A.S., et al. "Diagnosis and management of tickborne rickettsial diseases: Rocky Mountain spotted fever, ehrlichioses and anaplasmosis—United States." *Morbidity and Mortality Weekly Report* 55 (2006): RR–4.

Clements, M.L., et al. "Reactogenicity, immunogenicity, and efficacy of a chick embryo cell-derived vaccine for Rocky Mountain spotted fever." *Journal of Infectious Diseases* 148 (1983): 922–930.

Davidson, M.G., et al. "Vascular permeability and coagulation during *Rickettsia rickettsii* infection in dogs." *American Journal of Veterinary Research* 51 (1990): 165–170.

Demma, L.J., et al. "Rocky Mountain spotted fever from an unexpected tick vector in Arizona." *New England Journal of Medicine* 353 (2005): 587–593.

Diaz, C.M., et al. "Identification of protective components of two major outer membrane proteins of spotted fever group rickettsiae." *American Journal of Tropical Medicine and Hygiene* 65 (2001): 371–378.

Duma, R.J., et al. "Epidemic typhus in the United States associated with flying squirrels." *Journal of the American Medical Association* 245 (1981): 2318–2323.

Dumler, J.S. "Fatal Rocky Mountain spotted fever in Maryland." *Journal of the American Medical Association* 265 (1991): 718.

Dumler, J.S., and D.H. Walker. "Rocky Mountain spotted fever—changing ecology and persisting virulence." *New England Journal of Medicine* 353 (2005): 551–553.

Dumler, J.S., et al. "Rapid immunoperoxidase demonstration of *Rickettsia rickettsii* in fixed cutaneous specimens from patients with Rocky Mountain spotted fever." *American Journal of Clinical Pathology* 93 (1990): 410–414.

Elghetany, M.T., and David H. Walker. "Hemostatic changes in Rocky Mountain spotted fever and Mediterranean spotted fever." *American Journal of Clinical Pathology* 112 (1999): 159–168.

Eremeeva, M.E., and D.J. Silverman. "Effects of the antioxidant α-lipoic acid on human umbilical vein endothelial cells infected with *Rickettsia rickettsii.*" *Infection and Immunity* 66 (1998): 2290–2299.

Eremeeva, M.E., G.A. Dasch, and D.J. Silverman. "Quantitative analyses of variations in the injury of endothelial cells elicited by 11 isolates of *Rickettsia rickettsii.*" *Clinical Diagnostic Lab Immunology* 8 (2001): 788–795.

# Bibliography

Feng, H-M, and David H. Walker. "Mechanisms of intracellular killing of *Rickettsia conorii* in infected human endothelial cells, hepatocytes, and macrophages." *Infection and Immunity* 68 (2000): 6729–6736.

Feng, H-M, et al. "Fc-dependent polyclonal antibodies and antibodies to outer membrane proteins A and B, but not to lipopolysaccharide protect SCID mice against fatal *Rickettsia conorii* infection." *Infection and Immunity* 72 (2004): 2222–2228.

Feng, H-M, V.L. Popov, and David H. Walker. "Depletion of gamma interferon and tumor necrosis factor alpha in mice with *Rickettsia conorii*-infected endothelium: Impairment of rickettsicidal nitric oxide production resulting in fatal, overwhelming rickettsial disease." *Infection and Immunity* 62 (1994): 1952–1960.

Gage, K.L., W. Burgdorfer, and C.E. Hopla. "Hispid cotton rats (*Sigmodon hispidus*) as a source for infecting immature *Dermacentor variabilis* (Acari: Ixodidae) with *Rickettsia rickettsii*." *Journal of Medical Entomology* 27 (1990): 615–619.

Galvao, M., et al. "Fatal spotted fever rickettsiosis, Minas Gerais, Brazil." *Emerging Infectious Diseases* 9 (2004): 1402–1405.

Gilmore, R.D. Jr. "Comparison of the *rompA* gene repeat regions of *Rickettsiae* reveals species-specific arrangements of individual repeating units." *Gene* 125 (1993): 97–102.

Harden, V.A. "Koch's postulates and the etiology of rickettsial diseases." *Journal of the History of Medicine and Allied Sciences* 42 (1987): 277–295.

Harrell, G.T., and J.K. Aikawa. "Pathogenesis of circulatory failure in Rocky Mountain spotted fever. Alterations in the blood volume and the thiocyanate space at various stages of the disease." *Archives of Internal Medicine* 83 (1949): 331–347.

Hattwick, M.A.W., R.J. O'Brien, and B.F. Hanson. "Rocky Mountain spotted fever: Epidemiology of an increasing problem." *Annals of Internal Medicine* 84 (1976): 732–739.

Heinzen, R.A., S.F. Hayes, M.G. Peacock, and T. Hackstadt. "Directional actin polymerization associated with spotted fever group rickettsia infection of Vero cells." *Infection and Immunity* 61 (1993): 1926–1935.

Heinzen, R.A., S.S. Grieshaber, L.S. Van Kirk, and C.J. Dewin. "Dynamics of actin-based movement of *Rickettsia rickettsii* in vero cells." *Infection and Immunity* 67 (1999): 4201–4207.

Helmick, C.G., K.W. Bernard, and L.J. D'Angelo. "Rocky Mountain spotted fever: Clinical, laboratory, and epidemiological features of 262 cases." *Journal of Infectious Diseases* 150 (1984): 480–488.

Herrero-Herrero, J.I., D.H. Walker, and R. Ruiz-Beltran. "Immunohistochemical evaluation of the cellular immune response to *Rickettsia conorii* in *taches noires*." *Journal of Infectious Diseases* 155 (1987): 802–805.

Ismail, N., et al. "Current status of immune mechanisms of killing of intracellular microorganisms." *FEMS Microbiology Letters* 207 (2002): 111–120.

Johnson, J.E., and P.J. Kadull. "Rocky Mountain spotted fever acquired in a laboratory." *New England Journal of Medicine* 277 (1967): 842–847.

Kaplowitz, L.G., and G.L. Robertson. "Hyponatremia in Rocky Mountain spotted fever: Role of antidiuretic hormone." *Annals of Internal Medicine* 98 (1983): 334–335.

Kaplowitz, L.G., J.J. Fischer, and P.F. Sparling. "Rocky Mountain spotted fever: A clinical dilemma." *Current Clinical Topics in Infectious Diseases* 2 (1981): 89–108.

Kaplowitz, L.G., et al. "Correlation of rickettsial titers, circulating endotoxin, and clinical features in Rocky Mountain spotted fever." *Archives of Internal Medicine* 143 (1983): 1149–1151.

Kenyon, R.H., R.G. Williams, C.N. Oster, and C.E. Pedersen Jr. "Prophylactic treatment of Rocky Mountain spotted fever." *Journal of Clinical Microbiology* 8 (1978): 102–104.

LaScola, B., and D. Raoult. "Laboratory diagnosis of rickettsioses: Current approaches to diagnosis of old and new rickettsial diseases." *Journal of Clinical Microbiology* 35 (1997): 2715–2727.

Lillie, R.D. "The pathology of Rocky Mountain spotted fever." *National Institutes of Health Bulletin* 177 (1941): 1–46.

Marin-Garcia, J., and F.F. Barrett. "Myocardial function in Rocky Mountain spotted fever: Echocardiographic assessment." *American Journal of Cardiology* 51 (1983): 341–343.

Martinez, J.J., and P. Cossart. "Early signaling events involved in the entry of *Rickettsia conorii* into mammalian cells." *Journal of Cell Science* 117 (2004): 5097–5106.

Martinez, J.J., S. Seveau, E. Veiga, S. Matsuyama, and P. Cossart. "Ku70, a component of DNA-dependent protein kinase, is a mammalian receptor for *Rickettsia conorii*." *Cell* 123 (2005): 1013–1023.

# Bibliography

Maxey, E.E. "Some observations on the so-called spotted fever of Idaho." *Medical Sentinel* 7 (1899): 433–438.

McDade, J.E. "Evidence supporting the hypothesis that rickettsial virulence factors determine the severity of spotted fever and typhus group infections." *Annals of New York Academic Sciences* 590 (1990): 20–26.

McDade, J.E., and V.F. Newhouse. "Natural history of *Rickettsia rickettsii.*" *Annual Review of Microbiology* 40 (1986): 287–309.

McDade, J.E., C.C. Shepard, M.A. Redus, V.F. Newhouse, and J.D. Smith. "Evidence of *Rickettsia prowazekii* infections in the United States." *American Journal of Tropical Medicine and Hygiene* 29 (1980): 277–284.

MMWR. "Fatal cases of Rocky Mountain spotted fever in family clusters—Three states, 2003." *Morbidity and Mortality Weekly Report: CDC Surveillance Summaries/Centers for Disease Control* 53 (2004): 1–4.

Niebylski, M.L., et al. "*Rickettsia peacockii* sp. nov., a new species infecting wood ticks, *Dermacentor andersoni,* in western Montana." *International Journal of Systematic Bacteriology* 47 (1997): 446–452.

Niebylski, M.L., M.G. Peacock, and T.G. Schwan. "Lethal effect of *Rickettsia rickettsii* on its tick vector (*Dermacentor andersoni*)." *Applied Environmental Microbiology* 65 (1999): 773–778.

Ogata, H., et al. "Mechanisms of evolution in *Rickettsia conorii* and *R. prowazekii.*" *Science* 293 (2001): 2093–2098.

Paddock, C.D., et al. "Hidden mortality attributable to Rocky Mountain spotted fever: Immunohistochemical detection of fatal, serologically unconfirmed disease." *Journal of Infectious Diseases* 179 (1999): 1469–1476.

Paddock, C.D., et al. "*Rickettsia parkeri*: A newly recognized cause of spotted fever rickettsiosis in the United States." *Clinical Infectious Diseases* 38 (2004): 805–811.

Paddock, C.D., R.C. Holman, J.W. Krebs, and J.E. Childs. "Assessing the magnitude of fatal Rocky Mountain spotted fever in the United States: Comparison of two national data sources." *American Journal of Tropical Medicine and Hygiene* 67 (2002): 349–354.

Parker, R.R. "Rocky Mountain spotted fever: Results of fifteen years' prophylactic vaccination." *American Journal of Tropical Medicine and Hygiene* 21 (1941): 369–383.

Philip, R.N., et al. "*Rickettsia bellii* sp. nov.: A tick-borne rickettsia, widely distributed in the United States, that is distinct from the spotted fever

and typhus biogroups." *International Journal of Systematic Bacteriology* 33 (1983): 94–106.

Raoult, D., and M. Drancourt. "Antimicrobial therapy of rickettsial diseases." *Antimicrobial Agents and Chemotherapy* 35 (1991): 2457–2462.

Raoult, D., and V. Roux. "Rickettsioses as paradigms of new or emerging infectious diseases." *Clinical Microbiology Reviews* 10 (1997): 694–719.

Raoult, D., et al. "*Rickettsia africae*, a tick-borne pathogen in travelers to sub-Saharan Africa." *New England Journal of Medicine* 344 (2001): 1501–1510.

Ricketts, H.T. "The study of Rocky Mountain spotted fever (tick fever?) by means of animal inoculations: A preliminary communication." *Journal of the American Medical Association* 47 (1906): 33–36.

Ricketts, H.T. "The transmission of Rocky Mountain spotted fever by the bite of the wood-tick (*Dermacentor occidentalis*)." *Journal of the American Medical Association* 47 (1906): 358.

Ricketts, H.T., and R.M. Wilder. "The etiology of the typhus fever (tabardillo) of Mexico City." *Journal of the American Medical Association* 104 (1910): 1373–1375.

Ricketts, H.T., and R.M. Wilder. "The transmission of the typhus fever of Mexico (tabardillo) by means of the louse (*Pediculus vestamenti*)." *Journal of the American Medical Association* 104 (1910): 1304–1306.

Rydkina, E., A. Sahni, D.J. Silverman, and S.K. Sahni. "*Rickettsia rickettsii* infection of cultured human endothelial cells induces heme oxygenase 1 expression." *Infection and Immunity* 70 (2002): 4045–4052.

Rydkina, E., et al. "Selective modulation of antioxidant enzyme activities in host tissues during *Rickettsia conorii* infection." *Microbial Pathogen* 36 (2004): 293–301.

Sahni, S.K., et al. "Proteasome-independent activation of nuclear factor kB in cytoplasmic extracts from human endothelial cells by *Rickettsia rickettsii.*" *Infection and Immunity* 66 (1998): 1827–1833.

Saslaw, S., and H.N. Carlisle. "Aerosol infection of monkeys with *Rickettsia rickettsii.*" *Bacteriological Reviews* 30 (1966): 636–644.

Schmaier, A.H., et al. "Hemostatic/fibrinolytic protein changes in C3H/HeN mice infected with *Rickettsia conorii*—A model for Rocky Mountain spotted fever." *Thrombosis and Haemostasis* 86 (2001): 871–879.

Sexton, D.J., and G.R. Corey. "Rocky Mountain spotless and almost spotless fever: A wolf in sheep's clothing." *Clinical Infectious Diseases* 15 (1992): 439–448.

# Bibliography

Silverman, D.J., and C.L. Wisseman Jr. "Comparative ultrastructural study on the cell envelopes of *Rickettsia prowazekii*, *Rickettsia rickettsii*, and *Rickettsia tsutsugamushi.*" *Infection and Immunity* 21 (1978): 1020–1023.

Silverman, D.J., and L.A. Santucci. "Potential for free radical-induced lipid peroxidation as a cause of endothelial cell injury in Rocky Mountain spotted fever." *Infection and Immunity* 56 (1988): 3110–3115.

Silverman, D.J., C.L. Wisseman Jr., A.D. Waddell, and M. Jones. "External layers of *Rickettsia prowazekii* and *Rickettsia rickettsii*: Occurrence of a slime layer." *Infection and Immunity* 22 (1978): 233–246.

Spencer, R.R., and R.R. Parker. "Rocky Mountain spotted fever: Infectivity of fasting and recently fed ticks." *Public Health Report* 38 (1923): 333–339.

Teysseire, N., C. Chiche-Portiche, and D. Raoult. "Intracellular movements of *Rickettsia conorii* and *R. typhi* based on actin polymerization." *Research in Microbiology* 143 (1992): 821–829.

Thorner, A.R., D.H. Walker, and W.A. Petri Jr. "Rocky Mountain spotted fever." *Clinical Infectious Diseases* 27 (1998): 1353–1360.

Topping, N.H. "Rocky Mountain spotted fever: Further experience in the therapeutic use of immune rabbit serum." *Public Health Report* 58 (1943): 757–775.

Tzianabos, T., B.E. Anderson, and J.E. McDade. "Detection of *Rickettsia rickettsii* DNA in clinical specimens by enzymatic amplification using polymerase chain reaction technology." *Annals of New York Academic Sciences* 590 (1990): 553–556.

Valbuena, G., and David H. Walker. "Changes in the adherens junctions of human endothelial cells infected with spotted fever group rickettsiae." *Virchows Archiv* 446 (2005): 379–382.

Valbuena, G., H-M Feng, and David H. Walker. "Mechanisms of immunity against rickettsiae. New perspectives and opportunities offered by unusual intracellular parasites." *Microbes and Infection* 4 (2002): 625–633.

Valbuena, G., J.M. Jordan, and David H. Walker. "T cells mediate cross-protective immunity between spotted group rickettsiae and spotted fever group rickettsiae." *Journal of Infectious Diseases* 190 (2004): 1221–1227.

Vishwanath, S. "Antigenic relationships among the rickettsiae of the spotted fever and typhus groups." *FEMS Microbiology Letters* 81 (1991): 341–344.

Walker, David H. "Rocky Mountain spotted fever: A seasonal alert." *Clinical Infectious Diseases* 20 (1995): 1111–1117.

Walker, David H. "Ricketts creates rickettsiology, the study of vector-borne obligately intracellular bacteria." *Journal of Infectious Diseases* 189 (2004): 938–955.

Walker, David H. "Targeting *Rickettsia*." *New England Journal of Medicine* 354 (2006): 1418–1420.

Walker, David H. "Principles of the malicious use of infectious agents to create terror: Reasons for concern for organisms of the genus *Rickettsia*." *Annals of New York Academic Sciences* 990 (2003): 739–742.

Walker, David H. "Rickettsial diseases in travelers." *Travel Medicine and Infectious Diseases* 1 (2003): 35–40.

Walker, David H. "The role of host factors in the severity of spotted fever and typhus rickettsioses." *Annals of New York Academic Sciences* 590 (1990): 10–19.

Walker, David H., and Yu X-J. "Progress in rickettsial genome analysis from pioneering of *Rickettsia prowazekii* to the recent *Rickettsia typhi*." *Annals of New York Academic Sciences* 1063 (2003): 13–25.

Walker, David H., C.G. Crawford and B.G. Cain. "Rickettsial infection of the pulmonary microcirculation: The basis for interstitial pneumonitis in Rocky Mountain spotted fever." *Human Pathology* 11 (1980): 263–272.

Walker, David H., et al. "Fulminant Rocky Mountain spotted fever. Its pathologic characteristics associated with glucose-6-phosphate dehydrogenase deficiency." *Archives of Pathology Laboratory Medicine* 107 (1983): 121–125.

Walker, David H., G.A. Valbuena, and J.P. Olano. "Pathogenic mechanisms of diseases caused by *Rickettsia*." *Annals of New York Academic Sciences* 990 (2003): 1–11.

Walker, David H., J.P. Olano, and H-M Feng. "Critical role of cytotoxic T lymphocytes in immune clearance of rickettsial infection." *Infection and Immunity* 69 (2001): 1841–1846.

Walker, T.S. "Rickettsial interactions with human endothelial cells in vitro: Adherence and entry." *Infection and Immunity* 44 (1984): 205–210.

Wood, D.O., and A.F. Azad. "Genetic manipulation of rickettsiae: A preview." *Infection and Immunity* 68 (2001): 6091–6093.

Woodward, T.E. "A historical account of the rickettsial diseases with a discussion of unsolved problems." *Journal of Infectious Diseases* 127 (1973): 583–594.

# Bibliography

Zavala-Castro, J.E., et al. "Fatal human infection with *Rickettsia rickettsii* in Yucatán, Mexico." *Emerging Infectious Diseases* 12 (2006): 672–674.

Zinsser, H., and M.R. Castaneda. "On the isolation from a case of Brill's disease of a typhus strain resembling the European type." *New England Journal of Medicine* 209 (1933): 815–819.


Pertinent Web Sites

Centers for Disease Control and Prevention
**http://www.cdc.gov/ncidod/dvrd/rmsf/index.htm**

eMedicine
**http://www.emedicine.com/EMERG/topic510.htm**

MedlinePlus Medical Encyclopedia
**http://www.nlm.nih.gov/medlineplus/ency/article/000654.htm**

The Merck Manuals Online Medical Library
**http://www.merck.com/mmpe/sec14/ch177/ch177f.html?qt=rocky%20 mountain%20spotted%20fever&alt=sh**

New York State Department of Health
**http://www.nyhealth.gov/nysdoh/communicable_diseases/en/pdf/rocky.pdf**

Virginia Department of Health—Rocky Mountain Spotted Fever Fact Sheet
**http://www.vdh.state.va.us/epi/rmsff.htm**

# Index

engorged tick, 21–22, 78
epidemiology, 23–31, 78
eschar, 38, 44–45, 78
evolution, of rickettsiae, 12–14
eyes, as route of infection, 34

false negative, 57, 61
feeding, by ticks, 17–18, 20
Felix, A., 57
fever, 32
fibrin, 46, 78
flagella, 42, 78
Flinders Island spotted fever, 57
fluid, in lungs, 37
fluorescein, 60
fluoroquinolone, 65
folk customs, for tick removal, 69
Food and Drug Administration, 54
formaldehyde, 60
fulminant Rocky Mountain spotted fever, 39

gamma interferon, 48–49, 51, 78
gangrene, 39
gene amplification, 60–61
genes, rickettsial, 13–14, 63
genetic engineering, 74
gentamicin, 64
Gram-negative bacteria, 9, 14, 55, 78
guinea pig, 54, 56, 60, 69, 70
Gulf Coast tick, 38
gut barrier, 24

hard tick, 15, 19
headache, 32, 47
hemorrhage, 36, 45–46
host, 8, 78
host cell, 48

host protein, 41
hypothalamus, 47, 78

immune cells, 51
immune response, symptoms related to, 47
immune system, 40–41, 48–55
immunity, 10, 71, 78
immunofluorescent antibody assay (IFA), 58
incidence, 26, 78
incubation period, 32, 40
infection. *See also* reinfection; rickettsial infection
    alternate routes of, 34–35
    of endothelial cell, 46
    of ticks by *Rickettsia rickettsii*, 23–25
inflammation, lack of, from tick bite, 18
innate immunity, 48–49
inoculation, of bacteria into healthy cells, 8
insect repellent, 67
internal damage, 36–37
intracellular bacteria, 49
intravenous fluids, 65
Inuit people, 20
isolation of bacteria, for diagnosis, 56–57

Japan, biological weapons in, 75
Japanese spotted fever, 57

kidneys, 43–44, 65

larva (larval stage), 19, 23, 24
leukocytes, 48, 79
life cycle, of hard tick, 19
lipopolysaccharide, 53
louse-borne typhus, 52
lungs, 37
lymph, 40, 41

lymphatic vessel, 40
lymph nodes, 40–41
lymphocytes, 51–52
lysosome, 50, 53, 79

macrophage, 40, 51, 79
macules, 35–36, 79
maculopapule, 35–36
malaria, 38
Mediterranean spotted fever, 65–66
meningitis, 70
metabolism, of ticks, 20–22
mice, 53–55
microbial agent, 63
microtome, 60
minimal bactericidal concentration, 64
minimal bacteriostatic concentration, 64
mitochondria, 12–13, 79
molting, 19, 79
mountain goats, 20

Napoleonic Wars, 52
natural killer cells, 48–49, 79
necrosis, 43, 79
neutrophilic polymorphonuclear leukocytes, 48
newly discovered rickettsial diseases, 38
nidus, 68, 79
nymphal stage, 19, 23

obligate, 79
obligately intracellular bacteria, 14
organelles, 12–13, 42, 79
*Orientia tsutsugamushi*, 55
outcome, of illness, 37, 39
outer membrane proteins, 53, 54, 74
oxygen, 37, 43, 47, 65

painlessness, of tick bite, 17
Parker, R. R., 38, 69

penicillin, 63
perforin, 51, 79
phagocyte, 40, 80
phagocytosis, 50, 80
phagosome, 42, 50, 53
platelets, 46, 80
Poland, 52
polymerase chain reaction (PCR), 60–61
polymerization, 42, 80
population, of ticks, 30
preventive measures, 67–71
programmed cell death. See apoptosis
proteins, 41, 42. See also outer membrane proteins
*Proteus vulgaris,* 57, 61
Prowazek, Stanislaus von, 10

radiograph, 37
RANTES, 50, 80
rash, 34–36
receptor proteins, 41, 42
reemergence, of illness, 29–30
reinfection, 54, 55, 71
relatives, of *Rickettsia rickettsii,* 14, 44
removing ticks, 34, 67–69
renal failure. See kidneys
reproduction, of tick, 19
*Rhipicephalus sanguineus,* 15
ribosome, 63, 80
Ricketts, Howard T., 9–11, 56
rickettsia, 8–14. See also *Rickettsia rickettsii*
and immune system, 48–55
antibiotic action against, 63–66
antibiotic-resistant strains, 74

diagnosis, by seeing in tissue, 59–60
disease-causing mechanism of, 40–47
evolution of, 12–14
growing in laboratory, 11–12
origin of name, 9–10
related bacteria, 14, 44
*Rickettsia africae,* 38
*Rickettsia conorii,* 65–66
*Rickettsia honei,* 57
*Rickettsia japonica,* 57
rickettsial diseases, newly discovered, 38
rickettsial infection, 40–47, 52–55
*Rickettsia parkeri,* 38
*Rickettsia prowazekii,* 52–54, 73, 75
*Rickettsia rickettsii*
alternate routes of infection by, 34–35
as bioterror weapon, 73
as causative agent of illness, 8
cell wall structure, 53
infection of tick by, 23–25
isolation of, for diagnosis, 56–57
lack of antibioterrorism research on, 75
long-term effect on host tick, 23–24
natural ecology of, 23–31
spread of, between cells, 42
*Rickettsia slovaca,* 44
rickettsiostatic drugs, 63, 80
Rocky Mountain wood tick, 15, 18

saliva, of tick, 18, 21
salt, 20–21
satiated tick, 17, 80

Select Agents, 72–73
serological testing, 58–59
serology, 58
shock, 44
*Sigmodon hispidus,* 31
size, of rickettsiae, 14
skin, damage to, 35–36
skin biopsy, 60
Soviet Union, biological weapons in, 75
Spencer, Roscoe, 69
stabilizing, of patient, 65
stethoscope, 37
stupor, 37
sulfonamides, 66
symptoms, 32, 47

target cell, 41–42
T cell, 51
teeth, discoloration of, 64
terrorism. See bioterrorism
testing, of vaccines, 54
tetracycline, 63, 64, 70
tick, 15–22. See also *specific species, e.g.:* American dog tick
Clarence Birdseye's research, 20
blood feeding by, 17–18, 20
as culture vessels, 12, 69
infection by *Rickettsia rickettsii,* 23–25
life cycle of, 19
limiting exposure to, 67
long-term effect of *Rickettsia rickettsii* on, 23–24
metabolism of, 20–22
removing, 34, 67–69
various species, 15–16
tick-borne lymphadenopathy, 44–45
tick repellent, 67
tissue culture, 12
toxicity, of antirickettsial drugs, 64

# Index

**David H. Walker,** a native of middle Tennessee, has pursued a career in infectious diseases via the field of pathology since graduation from Vanderbilt University School of Medicine in 1969. His development as a pathologist studying infection and immunity was fostered by Drs. Gustave J. Dammin, Franz von Lichtenberg, and John Edgcomb investigating Chagas' disease at Harvard University, the Peter Bent Brigham Hospital, and the Gorgas Memorial Laboratory in Panama (1969-1973), and by Dr. Fred Murphy studying the pathogenesis of Lassa fever, lymphocytic choriomeningitis, and Venezuelan equine encephalitis at the Center for Disease Control (1973-1975). He embarked upon research in rickettsial diseases under the guidance of Dr. Charles Shepard and devoted 12 years while on the faculty of the University of North Carolina (1975-1987) to the study of Rocky Mountain spotted fever, boutonneuse fever, North Asian tick typhus and their etiologic agents in the laboratory and hospital in Chapel Hill and the field, hospitals, and laboratories in China and Sicily.

While serving as chair of the Department of Pathology, David H. Walker has developed infectious diseases as a research strength at the University of Texas Medical Branch at Galveston, founded the internationally recognized WHO Collaborating Center for Tropical Diseases, and heads the Center for Biodefense and Emerging Infectious Diseases. He does research supported by the National Institute of Allergy and Infectious Diseases, the Department of Defense, and the Clayton Foundation in the Rickettsial and Ehrlichial Diseases Research Laboratory, a team of scientists who investigate these microorganisms as well as their pathogenesis, diagnosis, epidemiology, and immunity, including projects to develop vaccines against rickettsioses and ehrlichioses.

As the pathologist member of an investigation team that went to Sverdlovsk, Russia, in 1992, he determined that the 1979 Sverdlovsk event was caused by inhalational anthrax. Subsequently, he has presented at the Food and Drug Administration related to approval of ciprofloxacin for prophylaxis and at the Institute of Medicine related to the ability of the anthrax vaccine to protect against inhalational anthrax.

Since January 2003, he has served as principal investigator of the Western Regional Center of Excellence in Biodefense and Emerging Infectious Diseases that involves more than 40 universities and other institutions in Texas, New Mexico, Oklahoma, Arkansas, and Louisiana. His department was the first at a university in the U.S. to operate a biosafety level-4 research laboratory.